Accounting for Non-Accountants

Accounting
For
Non-Accountants

A Manual
for Managers and Students

Third Edition

Graham Mott

**KOGAN
PAGE**

To Valerie

First published in Great Britain in 1984 by
Pan Books Limited.
Second edition 1988.
Third edition published in 1990 by
Kogan Page Limited, 120 Pentonville Road,
London N1 9JN.

British Library Cataloguing in Publication Data
A CIP record for this book is available
from the British Library.

ISBN 0-7494-0166-4

Printed and bound in Great Britain by
Richard Clay Limited (The Chaucer Press), Bungay

CONTENTS

Introduction

This book is written primarily for non-specialist students or managers who need to know about the financial workings of a firm. Accounting has a language of its own with a variety of statements and techniques which often mystify non-accountant colleagues. The aim of this book is to cut through as much jargon as possible and explain the various statements and techniques in a straightforward manner.

There are three parts to the book. The first deals with the types of statement found in the annual report. These include profit and loss account, balance sheet, value added, sources and applications of funds, inflation adjustments and performance ratios. Not only is the purpose of these statements explained but also the principles underlying their preparation. Guidance is given on both the use and the limitations of information contained in these reports.

The next section of the book starts to look inward at the more detailed operations of the firm. All the statements in the annual report relate to the whole firm and its historic performance. Managers need to know about the costs of products and the running costs of their departments. They are responsible for the cost of resources – men, materials, machines – under their control and must plan for their efficient future use. We therefore need to look at how firms cost products before progressing to the planning and control techniques of standard costing and budgetary control. Many decisions are based on an analysis of costs to determine the effects of changing the product mix, of closing down a department, of altering sales volume, whether to make or buy, to name but a few examples. All these decisions are based on the technique of marginal costing which uses the analysis of costs into fixed and variable categories.

The final part deals with the techniques of financial management which concentrate on the efficient use of capital. This embraces both the capital structure of the firm and the manner in which capital is invested in the assets of the business. The efficiency with which a firm carries out these operations is reflected in the profit and loss account and ultimately the share price if a private sector company. It also has wider ramifications for all companies in their ability to attract new capital and offer employment opportunities to existing and additional personnel.

Most of the book relates to any form of business organization, large and small, in both public and private sectors. Employees of nationalized industries will however find the chapters on share values and taxation largely irrelevant. That apart, the remaining chapters are as relevant to gas boards as they are to ICI or a local cooperative.

I have been very pleased at the take-up of this book on a wide variety of courses in the business and management field as well as its use by non-financial managers. In particular, I was pleased to see it included as recommended reading for the Institute of Marketing and the Certified Diploma in Accounting and Finance.

Graham Mott

Part 1
The annual accounts

1 Financial recording

Firms disclose financial information to outside parties at least once a year. There is no upper limit to the amount of information that can be provided to owners, employees, suppliers and others but minimum disclosure requirements are prescribed. These are found in various statutes and in a body of professional rules or standards.

The legal requirements on disclosure are contained in the Companies Act 1948, subsequently augmented in 1967 and 1981, now all consolidated into the Companies Act 1985. Listed or quoted companies also have to comply with Stock Exchange disclosure requirements. There is an obligation, though less specific, to inform employees of the financial results of their organization.

Not to be outdone, the accountancy profession produced the Corporate Report in 1975 which sets out a high standard of disclosure at which to aim. The profession exercises control with its 'statements of standard accounting practice', a list of which is contained in Appendix 6. There are also international accounting standards but these are unlikely to be more demanding than our own domestic variety.

These internal and external controls provide the framework within which accountants produce the detailed statements contained in a company's annual report. Before we look at these statements in subsequent chapters, we need to be aware of the conventions on which they are based and the ways that basic recording of transactions are performed.

Accounting conventions

Every business is regarded as a *separate entity*. If we wish to measure the performance of a business we need to keep its financial transactions separate from those of other businesses and from the personal transactions of its owners.

Accountants can only record transactions which have a *money measurement*. Money is the means of adding transactions together which is only possible when we can express transactions in money terms. For this reason a company's own goodwill never appears in the list of assets as its value is unknown until someone wants to take over the business and buy the goodwill. Only if we buy up another company and pay £X for its goodwill will it appear as a transaction.

The mythical man-in-the-street has usually heard of *double entry* bookkeeping and this term refers to the dual aspects of recording. By this is meant that every transaction has two aspects, a giving and a receiving aspect. These two aspects are recorded in separate accounts relating to the nature of the transaction. If the transaction is the payment of cash for wages then the two accounts involved are the cash account and the wages account. The same sum of money is entered in both accounts but the wages account receives the figure on the left (debit) side and the cash account gives the figure on the right (credit) side.

It might not seem very important to state exactly when income has arisen. If we sell goods on credit we can either say the sale takes place on delivery or when we receive the cash. The legal title to the goods usually passes on delivery and this factor determines in which month, or year, we say that income is realized or has arisen. We measure company performance over such discrete periods, therefore the *realization* concept places the sale in the correct period *matching* it up with the cost of the same goods.

In a similar way the *accrual* concept states that the expenditure incurred on earning the income is taken into account in that same period, irrespective of whether the cash has been paid out or not. The convention of *depreciation* is used to represent the notional amount a firm charges itself for the use of its own buildings and equipment.

When preparing financial statements the assumption of *continuity* is made; that the business is a 'going concern'. If a firm ceases to trade its possessions are sold off to the highest bidder but it would be very unlikely that they would fetch their cost price. Stocks of materials or part-finished work usually bring a smaller value in a liquidation than their worth to a continuing business.

Until very recently accountants only recorded transactions at their original cost to the firm. High rates of inflation in the 1970s have led accountants to amend the concept of *stability* of money as its value has been anything but stable in the last decade. We still record transactions at their original or historic cost but some firms additionally quantify the effects of inflation.

11

Sources of data

The source of all financial information is the document which originally records the transaction. Typical documents are timecards, stores issue notes and invoices. Accountants use a shorthand system called a 'cost code' to describe the nature of transactions. The cost code is constructed in sections with each section having a specific purpose. For example, blocks of numbers or letters may be used to describe the kind of expense or work carried out, which department did the work, who it was done for and possibly which physical asset was used. Use of cost codes allows a description of the transaction, and its value, to be fed into computer systems where it is sorted and stored until retrieved at a later date. An example of a cost code is shown in figure 1.1.

Figure 1.1 Typical cost code structure

2 7	5 6 4	8 3 7 2	1 0 6
Originating dept, cost centre or location number	Number describing the type of expense, the work done or source of income	Job, product or project number	Physical asset number, e.g. a machine or vehicle

A most important aspect of an accountant's job is his role of information manager. Not only does he manage information for his own use but he manages the information system used by all other managers and provides them with valuable data. If information is coded in the detail required, it is possible to recover basic information, or to present it in the form of a statement dictated by a computer programme. The assumption made here is that all but the smallest of businesses will have a computerized information system.

Recording transactions

If you have ever been the treasurer of a small club or society you most probably kept your financial records in a cash book, entering cash receipts on the left-hand page and cash payments on the right. A receipts and payments account is a summary of the cash book. The cash balance at the beginning of the year heads the receipts and the cash balance at the year end is the balancing figure between total receipts and total payments. A typical example is shown in figure 1.2

Figure 1.2 St Mary's Drama Club receipts and payments account 198X

Cash receipts	£	Cash payments	£
Cash balance at start	257	Hire of hall	50
Add:		Hire of costumes	180
Members' subscriptions	50	Refreshments	45
Sale of tickets	385	Printing and stationery	65
		Advertising	120
		Sub-total	460
		Cash balance at end	232
	£692		
			£692

Single entry bookkeeping

Many small businesses use a system of recording similar to the receipts and payments account. In their case a larger cash book is required with numerous columns to analyse the purposes of the receipts and payments. Figure 1.3 gives a simplified example of this approach.

Figure 1.3 Small company cash book

		Cash receipts					Cash payments			
Date	Description				Date	Description				
	Cash sales Credit sales Other receipts					Purchases Wages Office expenses Other payments				

The advantage of this system of recording is its simplicity, but there are some disadvantages. Most small businesses come within the VAT system when further analysis of sales and purchases will be required. The relevant tax point will not be when the cash receipt or payment is made but when the transaction was initiated.

Most firms buy and sell on credit so that payment is deferred a number of weeks from the date of purchase or sale. A statement of cash receipts and payments will not disclose the amount of money still owing to suppliers and bankers or that owed by customers. Nor is distinction made between cash spent on items consumed in the period and cash spent on items still having value remaining at the end of the period. We will therefore have to take account of these factors when preparing statements to measure company performance or to set out its financial position. This is explained in the next chapter.

Double entry bookkeeping

Most companies employing more than a handful of staff use a system of recording called double entry bookkeeping. This system records both *cash* and *credit* transactions on the principle that every transaction has two aspects. These are sometimes referred to as the giving and receiving aspects which in accounting terminology are called credits and debits respectively.

Taking a previous example of the payment of, say, £200 cash for wages, the two aspects are the firm giving cash and the employee receiving wages. In the old days when firms recorded such transactions in books and not on computer tapes or discs these two aspects would appear in the cash account and wages account as shown in figure 1.4

Figure 1.4 Sample accounts

Wages A/C		Cash A/C	
Cash 200			Wages 200

Receiving aspects (debits) are shown on the left side of an account and giving aspects (credits) are shown on the right side. No matter how many entries are made in numerous accounts the total of left-hand entries will always equal the total of right-hand entries overall. Each individual account, however, will not usually total the same figure on both sides. In this case there will be a balance on that account. These balances are listed in what is called a 'trial balance' to prove the numerical accuracy of recording, as debit balances must equal credit balances in total. We shall see in the next chapter that the trial balance provides the basic information for profit and loss accounts and balance sheets. Before we get to that stage let us record a few sample transactions using double entry principles:

Example

Joe Bloggs started up in business as a jobbing builder on 1 May and kept a record of the following transactions during his first month's trading. The names of the two relevant accounts are shown in the right-hand column:

Transaction	Accounts
1 May Opened bank account with £5,000 cash as his capital	Cash A/C Capital A/C
2 May Bought building plant for £500 cash	Plant A/C Cash A/C
2 May Bought building materials value £2,000 on credit from A. Supplier	Purchases A/C A. Supplier A/C
9 May Paid his staff £1,100 wages in cash	Wages A/C Cash A/C
16 May Paid his staff £1,200 wages in cash	Wages A/C Cash A/C
23 May Paid his staff £1,000 wages in cash	Wages A/C Cash A/C
30 May Paid his staff £1,000 wages in cash	Wages A/C Cash A/C
30 May Invoiced A. Customer for value of work done – £8,000	A. Customer A/C Sales A/C
31 May A. Customer paid £7,000 cash on account	Cash A/C A. Customer A/C
31 May Paid A. Supplier £1,800 on account	A. Supplier A/C Cash A/C

A number of different accounts are involved and these are shown at figure 1.5 in a T format with debits (receiving) on the left and credits (giving) on the right. Each transaction is entered twice in the two separate accounts with the name of the other account used for cross-reference. The balance on the account is shown as the circled amount and these balances make up the trial balance in figure 1.6.

At this point we have seen that the basic recording of transactions can be in one of two modes. Very small businesses tend to record only a single entry of cash transactions in a cash book. These are often described as incomplete records because the other aspect of each transaction is omitted, as are outstanding credit transactions. The other mode is to adopt double entry principles when credit and

15

Figure 1.5 Account entries for Joe Bloggs

Cash A/C

1 May	Capital	5,000	2 May	Plant	500
31 May	A. Customer	7,000	9 May	Wages	1,100
			16 May	Wages	1,200
			23 May	Wages	1,000
			30 May	Wages	1,000
Balance 5,400			31 May	A. Supplier	1,800

Purchases A/C

2 May	A. Supplier	2,000	
Balance 2,000			

Wages A/C

9 May	Cash	1,100	
16 May	Cash	1,200	
23 May	Cash	1,000	
30 May	Cash	1,000	
Balance 4,300			

Capital A/C

		1 May	Cash	5,000
		Balance 5,000	

Plant A/C

2 May	Cash	500	
Balance 500			

A. Supplier A/C

31 May	Cash	1,800	2 May	Purchases	2,000
			Balance 200		

A. Customer A/C

30 May	Sales	8,000	31 May	Cash	7,000
Balance 1,000					

Sales A/C

		30 May	A. Customer	8,000
		Balance 8,000	

Figure 1.6 Trial balance as at 31 May

Cash A/C	5,400	Capital A/C	5,000
Purchases A/C	2,000	A. Supplier A/C (creditor)	200
Wages A/C	4,300	Sales A/C	8,000
Plant A/C	500		
A. Customer A/C (debtor)	1,000		
	£13,200		£13,200

cash transactions are entered twice under relevant account headings. Whichever system is adopted it is possible to produce a profit and loss account and balance sheet as the next chapter explains.

Further reading

Business Accounting, I. F. Wood, Pitman.

Self-check questions

1 List as many as you can of the accounting conventions on which financial recording is based.
2 Design a cost code for your own firm.
3 Prepare a receipts and payments account from the following information for Gosforth Gardeners Association, showing the cash balance at the end of the year:

(1) Cash at start of year	£1,270
(2) Bulk purchase of seeds and fertilizers	£2,510
(3) Members' annual subscriptions	£560
(4) Sales of seeds and fertilizers to members	£2,250
(5) Purchase of equipment for hire	£1,500
(6) Hire fees received	£450

4 Prepare T accounts and a trial balance for John Deel, a market trader, who has provided you with the following information for his first year in business:

(1) Opened a business bank account with £1,500 of his own capital.
(2) Paid £1,200 for a stall and scales expected to last a number of years.
(3) During the year he purchased goods worth £17,000 from A. Wholesaler on credit.
(4) During the year he received £28,000 from cash sales to customers.

(5) He hired a van for business use at a cost of £300 per month inclusive of all running costs.
(6) During the year he withdrew £6,000 cash to live on (drawings A/C).
(7) Ignore stock and depreciation.
(8) Paid A. Wholesaler a total of £16,000 during the year.

2 Preparing annual accounts

Balance sheet

The annual accounts consist essentially of a balance sheet and a profit and loss account. The balance sheet is a snapshot picture at a moment in time. On the one hand it shows the value of assets (possessions) owned by the business and on the other it shows who provided the funds with which to buy those assets and to whom the firm is ultimately liable. Here we have an example of the dual aspects of recording which explains why a balance sheet must always balance. We can express this in the equation:

$$\boxed{\text{ASSETS}} \ = \ \boxed{\text{LIABILITIES}}$$

Assets are of two main types and are classified under the headings fixed assets or current assets. Fixed assets are the hardware used by the business and include buildings, plant, machinery, vehicles, furniture and fittings. These are assets the firm means to keep and are not the ones sold to customers. Other assets in the process of being turned into cash from customers are called current assets. These include stocks, work-in-progress, debts owed by customers and cash itself. Therefore we can say:

$$\boxed{\text{TOTAL ASSETS}} \ = \ \boxed{\text{FIXED ASSETS}} \ + \ \boxed{\text{CURRENT ASSETS}}$$

Assets can only be bought with funds provided by the owners or borrowed from someone else. Owners provide funds by directly investing in the business, say, when they buy shares issued by the company, or indirectly, by allowing the company to retain some of the profits. Therefore for a limited company:

$$\boxed{\text{SHAREHOLDERS' FUNDS}} \ = \ \boxed{\text{SHARE CAPITAL}} \ + \ \boxed{\text{RETAINED PROFITS}}$$

The same identity is true for non-incorporated businesses when the owner's capital comprises his initial investment plus any retained profits.

Borrowed capital can take the form of a long-term loan at a fixed rate of interest or may be a short-term loan like a bank overdraft or amounts owing to suppliers (creditors). These short-term debts are classified under the heading of current liabilities. Therefore:

$$\boxed{\text{BORROWED CAPITAL}} = \boxed{\text{LONG-TERM LOANS}} + \boxed{\text{CURRENT LIABILITIES}}$$

Having identified all the items in a balance sheet the total picture can be shown at any moment in time as in figure 2.1.

Figure 2.1 Balance sheet structure

SHAREHOLDERS' FUNDS	FIXED ASSETS
Share capital Retained profits	Buildings Plant and machinery Motor vehicles Fixtures and fittings
+ LONG-TERM LOANS	
+ CURRENT LIABILITIES	+ CURRENT ASSETS
Creditors (owing to suppliers) Bank overdraft	Stocks and work-in-progress Debtors (customers' debts) Cash
= TOTAL LIABILITIES	= TOTAL ASSETS

Taking the corporate sector as a whole, retained profit is a most important source of new capital for UK companies, accounting for 30% of requirements in some years. It is therefore a prime source of funds from which additional assets and growth are financed. However when losses occur this reduces both the value of the assets and

Figure 2.2 Effect of profit or loss on balance sheet

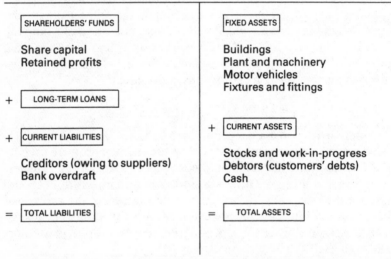

the shareholders' funds. We can depict the changes in a balance sheet by the amount of retained profit or loss for the year as in figure 2.2.

Profit and loss account

We now need to examine exactly what is meant by a profit or a loss. A profit and loss account is a summary of the firm's trading income from its customers, offset by its running expenses for the same period incurred on the goods or services sold. Therefore:

$$\boxed{\text{INCOME}} \quad - \quad \boxed{\text{EXPENSES}} \quad = \quad \boxed{\text{PROFIT (OR LOSS)}}$$

Income is defined as sales to customers and also includes rent or investment income received. The realization convention states that we count income when delivery takes place not when the actual cash is received from credit sales. For example, if sales were £120,000 during the year whilst cash received by the year end was £110,000 it is the former figure which counts as income.

Expenses are the cost of wages, materials and overheads used up during the year on the goods or services sold to customers. There are two tests as to whether an expense goes into the profit and loss account. First, it must relate to the time period covered by the statement irrespective of whether the cash payment has been completed. Secondly, the expense must relate to goods and services included as income in the same statement. Expenses incurred for a later period, or on goods or services not yet sold, go into the balance sheet as current assets.

All financial transactions are not immediately settled in cash because credit is both received and allowed in most industries. Notwithstanding these time lags it is useful at this stage to emphasize that all cash transactions do not go into the profit and loss account but some go into the balance sheet. Examples are cash received as extra loan or share capital, or money spent on new fixed assets like buildings or machinery. Figure 2.3 shows this distinction between so-called revenue and capital transactions.

It is a common misconception to think of the profit and loss account as a summary of all cash flowing into and out of the business, and that the excess of cash receipts over payments represents the profit. Such thinking ignores cash transactions in the

Figure 2.3 Cash flows affecting profit and loss account and balance sheet

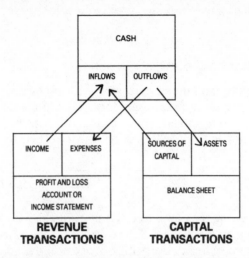

balance sheet, as when a company receives a loan from a bank. This is a cash receipt but cannot be counted as income in the profit and loss account as it must be repaid at some future date. Therefore the cash balance at any time bears no direct relationship to the profit or loss as a statement of sources and applications of funds later explains.

Having briefly defined the contents of a profit and loss account and balance sheet we can now see how these statements are prepared from the recorded transactions. All but the smallest firms record their financial transactions on double entry lines from which they prepare a trial balance as explained in the previous chapter. Balances on the left-hand side are called debit balances and can only be expenses or assets. The expenses go into the profit and loss account whilst assets are entered in the balance sheet. Right-hand balances in the trial balance are called credit balances and these must be either income or sources of capital (liabilities). We can therefore show the trial balance to be made up of two lists of balances which form the detailed entries in the profit and loss account or balance sheet as figure 2.4 portrays.

Figure 2.5 is the trial balance which first appeared as figure 1.6 in the previous chapter.

We can use these figures to produce a simple profit and loss account and balance sheet. This must also balance because the only additional figure of profit appears on the debit side of one statement and the credit side of the other. The resultant annual accounts are shown in figure 2.6.

22

Figure 2.4

Trial balance

Debit Balances	Credit Balances	
Expenses →	← Income	= Profit and loss A/C
or	or	
Assets →	← Sources of capital = Balance sheet	

Figure 2.5   Trial balance

Cash A/C	5,400	Capital A/C	5,000
Purchases A/C	2,000	A. Supplier A/C (creditor)	200
Wages A/C	4,300	Sales A/C	8,000
Plant A/C	500		
A. Customer A/C (debtor)	1,000		
	£13,200		£13,200

Figure 2.6   Joe Bloggs profit and loss account for May

Expenses	£	Income	£
Purchases	2,000	Sales	8,000
Wages	4,300		
Profit	1,700		
	£8,000		£8,000

Balance sheet as at 31 May

Assets	£	Sources of capital	£
Plant	500	Capital	5,000
Debtor (A. Customer)	1,000	Retained profit	1,700
Cash	5,400		
			6,700
		Creditor (A. Supplier)	200
	£6,900		£6,900

Note: Although not illustrated here the convention is to show the two sides of the balance sheet the opposite way around.

No matter how large an organization, these principles still apply, although a more detailed description of items will result in more complex statements than those appearing in figure 2.6. The legal form of a business organization will also affect the layout of the statement. These matters will be taken up later but the treatment of stocks, depreciation and credit transactions needs explanation now.

Stocks

In most businesses, goods purchased or manufactured are rarely all sold in the same accounting period and therefore give rise to stocks at the month or year end. A basic principle of the profit and loss account is that sales must be compared with the cost of goods sold and not with the cost of goods purchased. In ongoing companies we therefore have two stock figures to contend with – the opening stock at the beginning of the period and the closing stock at the end of that same period. Opening stock is an expense brought forward from a previous period to the present one, whilst closing stock is an expense to take from this period and carry forward to the next.

Let us assume that a firm sold goods for £50,000 one month when purchases cost £30,000. Stock at the beginning of the month was £12,000 and this had increased to £15,000 by the month end. Figure 2.7 shows one way of presenting this information as a 'trading account'.

Figure 2.7 Trading account showing the adjustment for opening and closing stocks

	£		£
Opening stock	12,000	Sales	50,000
Purchases	30,000	Closing stock	15,000
Gross profit	23,000		
	£65,000		£65,000

An alternative presentation of the same information brings out the cost of goods sold as a separate figure as in figure 2.8. It should be noted that the gross profit is identical with that in the previous layout of the same basic data.

Figure 2.8 Alternative treatment of stocks in the trading account

	£		£
Opening stock	12,000	Sales	50,000
Purchases	30,000		
	42,000		
less closing stock	15,000		
Cost of goods sold	27,000		
Gross profit	23,000		
	£50,000		£50,000

Depreciation

Figure 2.3 portrayed cash being spent in one of two ways – either on expenses or on assets. The expenses of labour, material and over-heads go into the profit and loss account, but not so the cost of fixed assets like vehicles or equipment. All may be thought of as neces-sary expenditure but the basic difference is time. Labour, material and overhead expenses are used up almost immediately unless expended on items still in stock. Fixed assets usually last for a number of years and it would be unfair to charge their whole acquisition cost in any one month or year. This problem is overcome by the simple expedient of charging a proportion of the cost, called depreciation, in the profit and loss account of each year of the asset's expected life.

Suppose a firm buys a machine for £10,000 and expects it to last five years after which time it will be scrapped. Each annual profit and loss account for the next five years will include £2,000 depreci-ation in its expenses. In the balance sheet each year the value of this machine will be reduced by a further £2,000 for every year which has passed, so that the values shown in figure 2.9 occur.

Figure 2.9

Balance sheet value at end of year:		Cost	Depn	Net
	1	10,000	2,000	8,000
	2	10,000	4,000	6,000
	3	10,000	6,000	4,000
	4	10,000	8,000	2,000
	5	10,000	10,000	*nil*

When the machine is scrapped it is omitted from the balance sheet list of assets, as it also would be if sold prematurely. In this latter case, any profit or loss arising on the sale would change the depreciation provision for the year on the remaining assets. The reasoning here is that a 'profit' is the result of charging too much depreciation in prior years and conversely a 'loss' is the result of charging too little. Depreciation is examined more fully in Chapter 4.

Debtors and creditors

In most industries credit is received from suppliers and granted to credit customers. Exceptions might be retail outlets with their cash sales, or the provision of personal services, where credit is not normally granted.

The conventions of realization and accrual state that income and expenditure are included in the profit and loss account statement if they relate to goods and services sold in that period, irrespective of whether the cash settlement has been finalized. In an annual profit and loss account, therefore, income will include credit sales for the last few weeks of the year and the amount outstanding appears as debtors in the list of current assets in the balance sheet. Similarly, expenses in the profit and loss account include goods and services bought in the latter part of the year but not yet paid for in cash. The amount owing to suppliers for these expenses, as well as for recent purchases for stock, will appear as creditors in the current liabilities section of the balance sheet. Conversely, any expenses like rent or rates which have been paid in advance appear as a debtor in the current assets but are excluded from this year's expenses shown in the profit and loss account.

Preparation of annual accounts from a trial balance

Having examined the treatment of stocks, depreciation, debtors and creditors we can now prepare a profit and loss account and balance sheet from a more comprehensive trial balance than that in figure 2.5.

The procedure is to identify items in the trial balance as appropriate to either the profit and loss account or balance sheet. Debit (left-hand) balances must be either expenses or assets whilst credit balances must be either income or sources of funds. In addition, information will normally be available about transactions which have not yet been recorded in the system and which are not included in the trial balance. The treatment of these 'adjustments' is outlined in figure 2.10 and they are always recorded twice to maintain the dual aspects of recording. One entry will be in the profit and loss account and the other entry in the balance sheet.

Example

The trial balance in figure 2.11 has been extracted from the books of Joe Brown, a trader, at 31 December 19X5. Prepare annual accounts from the information contained therein and incorporate the following adjustments:

(a) Depreciation of £1,000 is to be charged for the year.
(b) Stock at 31 December 19X5 was valued at £20,500.
(c) Rent and rates includes £750 paid in advance.

Figure 2.10 Treatment of adjustments in the annual accounts

	Profit and loss account		Balance sheet	
Adjustment	Income	Expenses	Sources of funds	Assets
Stock at year end	(Could show as income but more usual to reduce expenses)	Reduce purchases or relevant expense	—	Include in current assets
Depreciation provision for the year	—	Treat yearly amount as expense	—	Deduct cumulative total from asset
Payment in advance	—	Reduce relevant expense	—	Include with debtors in current assets
Provision for possible bad debts	Treat decrease as income	Treat increase as an expense	—	Deduct total provision from debtors

Figure 2.11　　　　　　　　Trial balance

	£		£
Equipment at cost	20,000	Owner's capital as at	
Stock as at 1 January	17,500	1 January	35,000
Debtors	8,000	Creditors	4,500
Cash and bank balances	3,000	Sales	70,000
Purchases	46,000	Depreciation as at 1 January	10,000
Salaries	9,000		
Rent, rates and insurance	4,000		
Miscellaneous expenses	3,500		
Drawings by owner	8,500		
	£119,500		£119,500

Profit and loss account for year ended 31 December 19X5

Expenses	£	Income	£
Stock at 1 January 19X5	17,500	Sales	70,000
add Purchases	46,000		
	63,500		
less Stock at 31 December 19X5	20,500		
Cost of goods sold	43,000		
Salaries	9,000		
Rent, rates and insurance	3,250		
Miscellaneous expenses	3,500		
Depreciation	1,000		
Net profit	10,250		
	£70,000		£70,000

(Continued overleaf)

Figure 2.11 continued

Balance sheet at 31 December 19X5

Sources of funds	£	Assets			£
Owners' capital at 1 January	35,000	*Fixed assets*	*Cost*	*Depn*	*Net*
add Profit for year	10,250	Equipment	20,000	11,000	9,000
	45,250				
less Drawings	8,500	*Current assets*			
Owners' capital at 31 December		Stock	20,500		
	36,750	Debtors	8,000		
		Prepayment	750		
Current liabilities		Cash and			
Creditors	4,500	bank	3,000		32,250
	£41,250				£41,250

Note: Assets and sources of funds are conventionally shown on the 'wrong' sides.

The following section relates only to the smallest businesses whose financial recording is not based on double entry principles. It should be ignored if only double entry is relevant.

Preparation of annual accounts from a cash book

Chapter 1 outlined the system of transaction recording favoured by very small businesses where transactions are entered in a cash book only when the receipt or payment is made. When preparing annual accounts from such a source the usual 'adjustments' will have to be made as when working from double entry records. These adjustments were set out in figure 2.10. However, further adjustments will have to be made in respect of credit transactions not completed at the year end. At the beginning of a year, some of the cash receipts and payments complete transactions initiated in the previous year. At the end of that year, some cash transactions will not be completed because of the period of credit granted and received.

For an ongoing company we therefore need to allow for these outstanding debtors and creditors when determining income and expenses for the year. The procedure is set out in figure 2.12.

Example

Joe Smith started up in business with £20,000 cash as his initial capital. He recorded his transactions in a cash book analysed into various columns according to their nature. Bills not yet paid were kept on a file separate from customers' invoices still outstanding.

Figure 2.12 Treatment of debtors and creditors when preparing annual accounts from a cash book

Adjustment	Profit and loss account		Balance sheet at year end	
	Income	Expenses	Sources of funds	Assets
Debtors (customers' debts) at start year	Deduct from this year's sales receipts			—
Debtors at end year	Add to this year's sales receipts			Include in current assets
Creditors (owing to suppliers) at start year		Deduct from payments for this year's purchases or other relevant expense	—	
Creditors at end year		Add to payments for this year's purchases or other relevant expense	Include in current liabilities	

During the year he arranged a bank loan to supplement his own capital. Prepare a profit and loss account for the year and a balance sheet at the year end. (A summary of the cash receipts and payments is also shown to illustrate the relationships.)

The layout of the profit and loss account and balance sheet in figure 2.13 leaves much to be desired. Related items like purchases and stocks appear in different places. By bringing together the items with common symbols we can summarize the transactions in the annual accounts shown in figure 2.14.

When the balance sheet proper is laid out in figure 2.14, which follows, the two items in figure 2.13 which are marked with the symbol * will be combined to show that the owner's capital has increased from £20,000 to £27,300 by the retention of profit during the year.

The two items with the symbol † attached will be combined in

Figure 2.13 Preparation of annual accounts from a cash book

	Cash flows		Profit and loss A/C		Balance sheet	
Cash transactions	Receipts	Payments	Income	Expenses	Sources of finance	Assets
1 Introduced £20,000 cash as initial capital	20,000				Capital 20,000*	
2 Purchase of equipment for £5,000 paid in cash		5,000				Plant and machy 5,000†
3 Purchase of goods for resale		110,000	Sales	Purchases 110,000		
4 Sales of goods	140,000		140,000		Loan	
5 Bank loan	4,000				4,000	
6 Wage payments to staff		20,000		Wages 20,000		
7 Other expenses paid		28,000		Expenses 28,000		
8 Interest charged on loan		200		Interest 200		
	164,000	163,200				
Cash and bank balance		800				Cash 800
	£164,000	£164,000				

Adjustments

	Cash flows		Profit and loss A/C		Balance sheet	
9 Bills unpaid at year end: £10,000 for purchases £2,000 for other expenses				Purchases 10,000 Expenses 2,000	Creditors 12,000	
10 Customers' accounts unpaid at the year end: £20,000			Sales 20,000			Debtors 20,000
11 Purchases unsold at year end: £18,500				Stock (—)18,500		Stock 18,500
12 Depreciation on equipment: £1,000				Dep'n 1,000		Depn (—)1,000†
Profit for year				Profit 7,300	Profit* 7,300	
			£160,000	£160,000	£43,300	£43,300

Note: Because this is a new business there are no debtors and creditors adjustments at the start of the year.

figure 2.14 to show that the value of the plant and machinery has depreciated from £5,000 to £4,000 at the year end.

Figure 2.14   Joe Smith profit and loss account for the year

	£		£
Purchases	120,000	Sales	160,000
less stock at year end	18,500		
Cost of goods sold	101,500		
Wages	20,000		
Other expenses	30,000		
Interest on bank loan	200		
Depreciation	1,000		
Profit for year	7,300		
	£160,000		£160,000

Balance sheet at the year end

Sources of funds		Assets			
	£				£
		Fixed Assets	Cost	Depn	Net
Owners capital*		Equipment†	5,000	1,000	4,000
Introduced at start	20,000	*Current assets*			
add Profit for year	7,300	Stocks	18,500		
	27,300	Debtors	20,000		
Bank loan	4,000	Cash	800		39,300
Current liabilities					
Creditors	12,000				
	£43,300				£43,300

Whether accounts are prepared from double entry records or a columnar cash book there is no difference in the final outcome. The detailed contents of the profit and loss account and balance sheet will be the same, irrespective of the type of basic recording used.

As mentioned previously, where the detail does differ is in response to the legal form adopted by a business organization. The next chapter explains these differences and looks at the format of published accounts.

Further reading

Business Accounting, I. F. Wood, Pitman.

Self-check questions

1 Prepare a profit and loss account and balance sheet from the following trial balance in respect of John Deel, a market trader. Allow for £400 depreciation on the stall and scales.

Cash A/C	£2,700	Capital A/C	£1,500
Equipment A/C	£1,200	A. Wholesaler	
Purchases A/C	£17,000	(creditor)	£1,000
Drawings A/C	£6,000	Sales A/C	£28,000
Van hire A/C	£3,600		
	£30,500		£30,500

2 Mr New started up as a jobbing builder on 1 January 198X with £5,000 in cash and no other assets or liabilities. At the end of his first year's trading he has prepared the following summary of his cash receipts and payments during 198X:

Receipts and payments 198X

Cash receipts	£	Cash payments	£
Cash introduced		Paid to builders merchants	20,000
as own capital	5,000	Wages, NHI, etc.	10,000
Received from clients	40,000	Purchase of van and plant	15,000
Loan from finance company	15,000	Interest on loan and overdraft	2,500
Bank overdraft at 31 December	3,000	Rent and rates	7,000
		Other expenses	8,500
	£63,000		£63,000

(a) State as many reasons as possible why the above statement is not a satisfactory explanation of Mr New's trading performance and financial position.

(b) Prepare a profit and loss account and balance sheet in the light of the following information:

    (1) Money owed by clients at 31 December was £10,000.

    (2) Money owing to builders merchants at the same date was £1,000.

    (3) Mr New valued his stocks and work-in-progress at £6,000 at the year end.

    (4) He also thought that his van and plant would last five years and should be written off over this period.

3 Presenting final accounts

For most practical purposes, the layouts of the profit and loss account for sole traders, partnerships, limited companies (and even public authorities) are identical. The exception comes at the very end of the statement which shows the disposition of the profit (or surplus) in taxation, rewards to the owners, and profit retained in the business. The layouts of the balance sheet are also nearly identical except for the section showing the owner's funds invested in the business. Assets owned by any type of business are capable of analysis into the now familiar fixed or current asset categories.

Let us take as an example identical basic information for the year ended 31 December 198X and see how it is treated in the different types of business organization. The data is:

	£
Capital originally introduced	30,000
Profit retained up to 1 January 198X	18,000
Net profit before tax for the year ended 31 December 198X	24,000
Tax due on profits	9,000
Personal drawings or dividends	10,000
Profit retained in the business	5,000

Self-employed

The sole trader or self-employed situation is the simplest. All the profit belongs to the one person and it is usual to show the profit before any personal drawings are charged. This accords with the profit which the Inland Revenue use to levy income tax, as otherwise, drawings would not be taxed. In the balance sheet the original capital and retained profit are merged into a combined 'capital account' which is reduced by any personal drawings of the proprietor. As income tax is levied on the owner rather than on the business it is not usually shown in the accounts but treated as drawings when actually paid.

Illustration

End of profit and loss account

	£
Net profit for the year	24,000

Balance sheet:
  Capital account

	£	
Balance at 1 January 198X	48,000	(30,000+18,000)
add Net profit for the year	24,000	
	72,000	
less Personal drawings	10,000	
Balance at 31 December 198X	62,000	

Note: The apparent increase in the owner's capital account will be reduced by further drawings at a later date when the £9,000 tax is paid leaving capital of £53,000 – an increase of £5,000.

Partnership

The partnership agreement, or in its absence the Partnership Act 1890, may allow for interest on the original capital, for the payment of salaries to partners, and state the proportions in which remaining profits are to be shared. Interest and salaries paid to partners are still regarded as shares of the profit for tax purposes. It is necessary to show these items in an appropriation section at the end of the profit and loss account together with the agreed division of remaining profit. Tax is dealt with in the same way as in sole trader's accounts. If interest is paid only on the original capital and not on profits retained in the business then it is necessary to have separate capital and current accounts for each partner in the balance sheet. In the following illustration it is assumed that the two partners A and B each receive salaries of £6,000 and £4,000 respectively; that 10% interest is allowed on their capital accounts and that any balance of profit is shared equally between them.

Illustration

End of profit and loss account			£
Net profit for the year			24,000
Interest on capital accounts	A	1,000	
	B	2,000	
Salaries	A	6,000	
	B	4,000	
Balance divisible equally	A	5,500	
	B	5,500	24,000

Balance sheet			£
Capital accounts	A	10,000	
	B	20,000	30,000

Current accounts	A	B	
Balance as at 1 January 198X	5,700	12,300	
add Interest on capital	1,000	2,000	
Salary	6,000	4,000	
Share on profit	5,500	5,500	
	18,200	23,800	
less Personal drawings	4,600	5,400	
Balance as at 31 December 198X	13,600	18,400	32,000

Note: The same principle applies here as in the note on self-employed, i.e. the apparent increase in the partners' current accounts will be reduced by further drawings of £9,000 when they make their personal tax payments. The increase in current account balances will then be £5,000 more than the figure at the start of the year.

Limited company

A company is a separate entity from its individual owners or shareholders so that corporation tax payable by the company is shown as an appropriation of profit together with the dividends paid and proposed for the year. Any balance of profit remaining, after tax and dividend have been provided, is not added to the original share capital but is shown as a 'revenue reserve'. Companies are legally obliged to show the issued share capital and reserves separately in their balance sheets, although together they form the total shareholders' funds invested in the business. Tax owing and dividends declared, but unpaid at the year end, appear as current liabilities. If the tax is not due within the next twelve months it is shown as a long-term liability.

Illustration

End of profit and loss account	£
Net profit for the year	24,000
Corporation tax payable on year's profit	9,000
Profit after tax	15,000
Dividends on ordinary shares	10,000
Retained profit added to revenue reserves	5,000

Balance sheet		
Authorized and issued share capital		£
30,000 ordinary shares of £1 each fully paid		30,000
Revenue reserves (retained profits)		23,000
Current liabilities		
Corporation tax payable	9,000	
Proposed dividend	10,000	19,000

Notes: The revenue reserve of £23,000 comprises £18,000+£5,000.
Corporation tax could be a long-term liability dependent on the due
date for payment and whether it is deferred. If an interim dividend has
been paid during the year only the proposed final dividend appears as
a current liability.

Public authorities

The income statement of a local authority or nationalized industry
takes the same form as a profit and loss account and is prepared on
the same principles and conventions. In the case of a local authority
a surplus would relieve the rate burden for local householders,
whilst a deficit would add to it. Local authorities' trading activities
are excluded from the corporation tax system but nationalized
industries are included. Provided taxable profits exceed capital
allowances on investment, nationalized industries are subject to
corporation tax like any private sector company. Profits are usually
retained within the industry to help self-finance new investment,
but on occasion dividends have been paid to central government.
The government is the owner of all the share capital and the
provider of some of the loan capital. There is nothing to stop a
nationalized industry tapping the commercial capital markets of the
world to supplement these domestic sources of capital. Interest
must be paid on loans irrespective of their source although it is more
difficult for a government to foreclose on a nationalized industry in
financial difficulty.

Layout of annual accounts

The profit and loss account has been shown to be a statement of income offset by expenditure on the other side, the difference between the two totals being the profit or loss for the period. Nowadays companies adopt the more modern layout of a profit and loss account by presenting it in a vertical format. A simple example of this is shown in figure 3.1 whilst a comprehensive model is shown in Appendix 1 at the end of the book.

Figure 3.1 Company profit and loss account in vertical format

	£'000
Sales	1,000
less Cost of sales:	
Purchases for resale or manufacturing costs (direct labour, direct materials and factory overheads)	600
Gross profit	400
less Administration, selling and distribution, finance costs	300
Net profit	100
less Taxation	40
Dividends	35
Retained profit	25

For internal consumption by management, full details of expenses are gradually deducted from income to show gross profit and finally the net profit. Strictly speaking what we are calling the profit and loss account comprises four stages as follows:

- Stage 1. Manufacturing A/C. If appropriate to the business this shows the cost of goods manufactured.
- Stage 2. Trading A/C. This shows the gross profit earned by matching the income against the cost of sales.
- Stage 3. Profit and loss A/C. The overhead expenses of running the business are deducted from gross profit to arrive at net profit.
- Stage 4. Appropriation A/C. This shows how the profit is appropriated in tax provisions, payments to owners and retention in the business.

Partnerships and self-employed persons do not have to disclose their accounts to any outsider other than the tax inspector. Not so limited companies. They must send annual accounts to their shareholders and file a copy at Companies House. Disclosure requirements vary according to the size of the company, as measured by turnover and number of employees. All companies need to make full disclosure to their shareholders but the smaller firms can withhold some information when filing their annual report at Companies House.

Companies are obliged to show details of a number of expenses, for example, depreciation, leasing payments, auditors' and directors' remuneration. They usually do this in notes accompanying the profit and loss account statement.

Alternative formats are available to cater for the widely varying activities of companies and one commonly used format is illustrated now in figure 3.2.

Figure 3.2 Published profit and loss account

		£000
	Sales	15,750
(−)	Cost of sales	10,500
(=)	Gross profit	5,250
(−)	Distribution costs	1,700
(−)	Administrative expenses	1,410
(+)	Other operating income	20
(=)	Operating profit	2,160
(−)	Interest payable	160
(=)	Profit on ordinary activities before tax	2,000
(−)	Tax on profit of ordinary activities	700
(=)	Profit for the financial year (earnings)	1,300
(−)	Dividends paid and proposed	550
(=)	Profit retained for the year	750
	Earnings per share	12.5p

Layout of the balance sheet

The word 'balance' in a balance sheet derives from the dual aspects of recording each transaction. The money which bought the various assets owned by the business is matched by the liability to repay the same sum to the various providers of capital. Therefore we are able to say liabilities equals assets when we list both aspects separately on the two sides of a balance sheet as follows:

Figure 3.3 Horizontal layout of a balance sheet

Liabilities	£000	Assets	£000
Shareholders' funds	82	Fixed assets	57
Long-term liabilities	18	Current assets	73
Current liabilities	30		
Total liabilities	£130	Total assets	£130

It is also possible to view current liabilities, not as a source of long-term capital, but as a short-term means of financing current assets. Amounts owing to creditors, shareholders and the taxman which are included in current liabilities are free sources of finance. These reduce the amount of shareholders' funds or loans which would otherwise be required. An alternative layout of a balance sheet shows current assets being partly financed by these current liabilities, with the remainder financed by long-term capital. The net figure of current assets after deducting current liabilities is called working capital – a term with which many non-accountants will be familiar but possibly could not accurately define. If this layout is adopted the balance sheet in figure 3.4 will result.

Figure 3.4 Alternative horizontal layout of a balance sheet

Sources of capital	£000	Assets		£000
Shareholders' funds	82	Fixed assets		57
		Working capital:		
Long-term liabilities	18	Current assets	73	
		less Current		
		liabilities	30	43
Capital employed	£100	Net assets		£100

It is common practice these days to use a balance sheet layout which can be shown on one page rather than the two pages which a horizontal layout necessitates. A vertical layout is the result, when assets are usually listed first and shown to be financed from the various sources of capital. It is also usual to bring out working capital in the vertical presentation so that the right-hand side of figure 3.4 is positioned above the left-hand side as figure 3.5 demonstrates.

Figure 3.5 Vertical layout of a balance sheet

		£000
Fixed assets		57
Current assets	73	
Creditors due within one year	(30)	
Net current assets (i.e. working capital)		43
Total assets less current liabilities		100
Creditors due after one year		(18)
Total net assets		82
Capital and reserves (i.e. shareholders' funds)		82

It must be stressed that all three presentations are correct as they all contain identical information. Most published accounts are in the vertical form described in figure 3.5 but we should be aware of the other possibilities from which it has been derived. A comprehensive example of the vertical layout is shown in Appendix 2.

Consolidated or group accounts

Shareholders of limited companies are not necessarily individuals. As a company is a separate legal entity it follows that it can be a shareholder in another company. When the shareholding exceeds 50% of the voting capital then that other company is called a subsidiary of the parent or holding company. This is very commonplace in the UK, where many public and private companies wholly, or partly, own other (subsidiary) companies. Each individual company must produce and distribute to its shareholder(s) a set of annual accounts. However, the various companies in a group are parts of one single undertaking. Consolidated accounts are the means of informing only the parent company's shareholders of the financial position and performance of all the companies which it controls. These take the form of a consolidated profit and loss account, a parent company balance sheet and a consolidated balance sheet, which are now explained in turn.

Consolidated profit and loss account

This statement combines all the separate profit and loss accounts of the parent and subsidiary companies. Where the subsidiary companies are wholly owned, then sales, trading profit, interest, tax, etc., are aggregated item by item. Sales to other group companies which have not been resold to third parties must be eliminated, as must any profits on such sales or interest on inter-group loans. The logic here is that a company cannot sell to, or profit from, itself.

In the case where all subsidiary companies are not wholly owned then all of the profit does not belong to the parent company. The proportion of the profit after tax belonging to the outside shareholders is deducted to arrive at the profit attributable to the parent company's shareholders. These outside or minority shareholders in subsidiary companies are called minority interests. An abbreviated example of a consolidated profit and loss account is shown in figure 3.6.

Figure 3.6 Example of a consolidated profit and loss account

		£
	Sales	10,000,000
(−)	Operating costs	9,533,000
=	Trading profit	467,000
(−)	Interest payable	53,000
=	Profit on ordinary activities before tax	414,000
(−)	Tax on profit on ordinary activities	140,000
=	Profit on ordinary activities after tax	274,000
(−)	Minority interests	15,000
=	Profit attributable to parent company	259,000
(−)	Dividends to parent company shareholders	57,000
=	Retained profit of parent company	202,000

Sometimes companies own strategic shareholdings in other companies which are less than 50% of the voting capital so that they are not classified as subsidiary companies. In this case the company in question is called a 'related company'. When producing a consolidated profit and loss account, the holding company must disclose its proportionate share in related company profits and losses, irrespective of whether or not it receives such profits as dividends.

Parent company balance sheet

This has all the appearance of a normal balance sheet except that included in the assets will be the cost of shares owned in subsidiary

41

(and related) companies plus any amounts owed by them. Conversely if the parent company has borrowed money from a subsidiary company this indebtedness will also be disclosed.

Consolidated balance sheet

A consolidated balance sheet is prepared by adding together the individual balance sheets of the parent company and its subsidiaries. This is achieved as follows:

1 All fixed and current assets and external liabilities are amalgamated item by item.
2 Inter-company indebtedness is eliminated.
3 The cost of the investment in subsidiary companies cancels out the proportion of the shareholders' funds acquired in those companies.
4 If there is an excess purchase cost over the value of shareholders' funds acquired, this is called goodwill. Conversely, a capital reserve occurs when the purchase cost is less than the value of shareholders' funds acquired.
5 The amount of shareholders' funds in subsidiary companies owned by outside shareholders is shown separately as 'minority interests'.

Example

The simplest situation is where a parent company (P Ltd) sets up a wholly owned subsidiary (S 100% Ltd) from the beginning. In this case there are no minority interests and no goodwill to concern us. The relevant balance sheets are set out in figure 3.7 together with the resultant consolidated balance sheet.

When a subsidiary company is only partly owned, then all the assets (less debts) are not owned by the parent company even though they are all shown in the consolidated balance sheet. Therefore the value of these assets, which equals the value of shareholders' funds owned by outsiders in the subsidiary company, is shown as a liability on consolidation. A further example is now taken of a parent company (P Ltd) owning 80% of a subsidiary company (S 80% Ltd) which was set up in conjunction with another company who provided the other 20% of the share capital. The relevant balance sheets are set out in figure 3.8 (page 44).

If the subsidiary was bought at a later stage then the cost of the investment must be matched against the value of shareholders' funds acquired, including the pre-acquisition profits held in

Figure 3.7   P Ltd balance sheet

	£000		£000
Issued share capital	22,000	Fixed assets	11,000
Reserves	1,300	Investment in S	
		100% Ltd	10,000*
	23,300	Loan to S 100% Ltd	2,000†
Current liabilities	1,200	Current assets	1,500
	£24,500		£24,500

S 100% Ltd balance sheet

	£000		£000
Issued share capital	10,000*	Fixed assets	17,300
Reserves	15,400	Current assets	21,100
	25,400		
Loan from P Ltd	2,000†		
Current liabilities	11,000		
	£38,400		£38,400

P Ltd consolidated balance sheet

		£000			£000
Issued share capital		22,000	Fixed assets	11,000	
Reserves	1,300			17,300	28,300
	15,400	16,700			
Current	1,200		Current assets	1,500	
liabilities	11,000	12,200		21,100	22,600
		£50,900			£50,900

Note: The items cross-referenced with symbols † and * cancel each other out in the consolidated balance sheet.

reserves. This comparison determines whether goodwill or a capital reserve arises on consolidation at the year end. Only post-acquisition profits in the subsidiary are included in the consolidated reserves. The distinction of profits of the subsidiaries into 'pre-' and 'post-acquisition' is also important for dividend purposes. The parent company must not pay dividends to its shareholders from pre-acquisition profits of subsidiaries. These matters are more complex than the purpose of this book allows us to pursue, so interested readers should follow them up elsewhere.

In this chapter we have examined the final accounts for differing types of organization and shown how the statements are usually

Figure 3.8

P Ltd balance sheet

	£000		£000
Issued share capital	30,000	Fixed assets	22,000
Reserves	15,000	Investment in	
	———	S 80% Ltd	20,000*
	45,000	Loan to S 80% Ltd	5,000†
Current liabilities	5,000	Current assets	3,000
	———		———
	£50,000		£50,000

S 80% Ltd balance sheet

	£000		£000
Issued share capital	25,000*	Fixed assets	35,000
Reserves	10,000		
	———		
	35,000		
Loan from P Ltd	5,000†		
Current liabilities	20,000	Current assets	25,000
	———		———
	£60,000		£60,000

P Ltd consolidated balance sheet

		£000			£000
Issued share capital		30,000	Fixed assets	22,000	
	15,000			35,000	57,000
Reserves (80%)	8,000	23,000			
		———			
		53,000			
Minority interests					
(20% × 35,000)		7,000			
Current	5,000		Current assets	3,000	
liabilities	20,000	25,000		25,000	28,000
		———			———
		£85,000			£85,000

Note: The inter-company loan cross-referenced † cancels itself out. The investment in the subsidiary of £20,000 cancels out 80% of the issued share capital of the subsidiary; the other 20% being part of minority interests.

presented in a modern format. We have also looked at the principle of consolidation because most published accounts of quoted companies represent the activities of a group rather than a single company. Now we need to look more carefully at the balance sheet detail.

Further reading

Business Accounting, I. F. Wood, Pitman.
The Meaning of Company Accounts, W. Reid and D. R. Myddelton, Gower.
The Structure of Consolidated Accounts, H. K. Jaeger, Macmillan.

Self-check questions

1 Why does a self-employed person not normally show drawings in his profit and loss account list of expenses?
2 Subject to any partnership agreement, in what ways may partners share out the profit between themselves?
3 Is the 'retained profit' for the year for a limited company the profit before or after charging tax and dividends?
4 What are the four sections or accounts into which a profit and loss account can be divided?
5 What is 'capital employed'?
6 Distinguish between fixed assets and current assets.
7 Define 'working capital'.
8 What are 'minority interests'?

4 Balance sheet details

Previous chapters have dealt with the preparation of balance sheets without going into too much detail about the constituents. This chapter looks in more detail at the two main sources of capital – owners' funds and borrowings – and the two main categories of possessions that they finance – the fixed and current assets. For the moment we are going to ignore the existence of inflation and concentrate on what is known as the 'historic cost' convention. In essence this means recording the original value of financial transactions and not updating for the effects of inflation. The following chapter deals with inflation and shows how we adjust annual accounts to allow for its impact.

Sources of funds

The two main sources of funds for a company are its shareholders (or owners) and its creditors. Each of these two sources can be further divided. The share capital provided by the shareholders when they purchase shares, and retained profits ploughed back in the business, both belong to the shareholders, but are generally shown separately in the balance sheet. Similarly, funds borrowed by the company are normally divided into 'long-term liabilities' which do not have to be paid back within the next twelve months, and 'current liabilities' which must be paid within the year. As we have seen, many firms show current liabilities as a deduction from current assets rather than as a source of funds.

Share capital

Ordinary shares form the bulk of the shares issued by most companies and are the shares which carry the ordinary risks associated with being in business (they are sometimes referred to as 'risk' capital), but expect to receive the bulk of the benefits when business is good. All the profits of the business including retained profits, not specifically allocated to other classes of share, belong to the ordinary shareholders. They have no fixed rate of dividend but many companies would hope to gradually increase the dividend payment over the years in line with the growth of company profits.

Preference shares are 'preferred' over ordinary shares in two ways. They receive their fixed percentage dividend before the ordinary shareholders receive any dividend, and are repaid their original investment before the ordinary shareholders in the event of the company being wound up. The precise rights and obligations attaching to a particular share can only be ascertained by reference to the company's memorandum and articles of association. Some preference shares, for example, are cumulative. This means that if the dividend is missed one year the right to receive it carries forward to future years when it may become possible to pay off the accumulated arrears. For tax reasons, preference shares are no longer a popular source of capital for companies who can alternatively borrow capital and obtain tax relief on the interest payment.

There can be other classes of share which, like any other saleable commodity, can be designed to appeal to different sectors of the market. One example would be a management share designed to pay a dividend only when profits exceeded a certain amount, i.e. a carrot intended to encourage senior management to aim for high profits. Another example would be a founder's share which carried more votes than ordinary shares, so keeping control in the founder's hands whilst allowing it to raise new capital by share issues. It should be pointed out at this stage that the Stock Exchange frowns on companies issuing ordinary shares with varying voting rights. Listed companies therefore do not have the freedom of unlisted companies in this respect.

A company does not have to issue all its share capital at once, nor does it have to obtain payment in full for each share it issues immediately. The total amount it is authorized to issue must, however, be shown as a note on the balance sheet next to the amount it has actually issued. These amounts are known as the 'authorized' and 'issued' capital respectively.

Partly paid shares are a rarity although one or two instances occurred during the late 1970s oil exploration boom. In this situation a shareholder's liability for the company's debts extends to the share capital not yet called up. Partly paid shares resulting from privatizations are a different case. Here the outstanding amounts are due to the government and not the company concerned.

Reserves

Reserves are normally divided into 'capital' reserves and 'revenue' reserves. Revenue reserves are those consisting of trading profits which have been retained in the business after payment of dividends and tax. Capital reserves, on the other hand, consist of special sorts of profits which do not arise out of normal trading. The essential difference in law is that revenue reserves can be used to pay dividends to the shareholders and capital reserves cannot.

One example of a capital reserve arises when a company sells its own shares at above their face value. Only the face value can be shown as share capital but the 'profit' made on the shares cannot be treated as a normal trading profit and paid out to the shareholders. It must therefore be held in the business as a capital reserve called 'share premium account'. Another example of a capital reserve is profit arising on the revaluation of a fixed asset.

It is most important not to confuse reserves (or profit generally) with cash. The firm has made a profit when its owners' net assets have increased, here defined as total assets less all external liabilities. If, for example, a firm started the year with £10,000 in cash and no other assets or liabilities, and ended the year with stocks worth £15,000 and no other assets or liabilities, it would have made a profit of £5,000 but would still not have any cash. Reserves reflect the fact that the net worth of the company has grown but does not specify in what form that increase in worth is held. One major problem faced by growing companies is that they are making profits, but these profits are all tied up in plant, machinery and stocks, leaving them without the cash to pay their creditors.

Long-term liabilities

Share capital is often referred to as 'permanent capital'. It is there as long as the company continues to exist. Very often the company needs funds for a long period of time but does not wish to commit itself to a permanent increase in its capital. In these circumstances it will borrow the capital required, particularly if it can use the funds to earn profit at a higher rate than the fixed rate of interest it pays the lender.

There are many means by which a company can borrow long-term funds. It can be done by mortgage, by arrangement with banks and insurance companies, and so on. Very often loans of this nature are secured by a general or floating charge on the assets or particular groups of assets of the company. Large companies of good standing can arrange to borrow without security and this is simply called an unsecured loan.

One of the commonest ways of raising long-term capital is by issuing debentures. A debenture is a document given by the company as evidence of debt to the holder(s) and entails certain obligations in relation to repayment of capital and payment of interest. It is important to appreciate that although in many ways debenture-holders might appear to be similar to shareholders, they are not part-owners of the company but are creditors. Payments of interest (not dividends) on the capital they have lent must be paid whether or not the company makes a profit.

Current liabilities

Current liabilities are in the main the liabilities the company incurs in the course of carrying on its normal trading. Examples are amounts owing to suppliers (trade creditors), amounts owing for services ('accruals'), bank overdraft, dividends proposed but not yet paid and tax due to be paid within the next year. As already indicated, it is increasingly common for current liabilities to be regarded as a 'negative' current asset in the working capital cycle and shown as a deduction from assets, rather than as a source of funds. This working capital cycle starts with creditors who supply raw materials which are turned into work-in-progress and then into finished goods, the finished goods are sold to debtors who eventually pay cash, which in due course is paid to suppliers. This is shown diagrammatically at the beginning of Chapter 15.

Other sources

Occasionally one hears of companies selling off their valuable premises to a financial institution or property company, but continuing to occupy them on a long-term lease. This is known as 'sale and leaseback' and is a once-and-for-all means of raising funds, either to acquire other types of fixed assets or to inject more working capital. Future profits from such new assets will be offset in the profit and loss account by the annual rent charge.

Other sources of finance for fixed assets rely on spreading the acquisition cost over a long period of time. Hire purchase ensures the company will be the eventual owner of the asset. The original capital cost is shown as a fixed asset and depreciated accordingly. The principal outstanding at the balance sheet date is shown as a liability or source of capital whilst the interest paid is written off as an expense in the profit and loss account each year.

Leasing is another alternative to paying for a fixed asset in full and avoids having to raise new long-term capital for that purpose. In recent years the leasing of equipment, vehicles and even furniture has become as commonplace as the renting of property with which it is analogous. Leasing payments, like rent, appear as expenses in the profit and loss account.

Mention was made earlier that current liabilities are often viewed as a part-financier of current assets, so reducing the amount of permanent working capital required to be financed by owners and borrowed capital. An appropriate source of funds for working capital is available from the factoring or discounting of sales invoices. Instead of having to wait perhaps up to two months for credit customers to pay, the bulk of the money can be obtained from the finance company immediately. Discounting is when a company merely gets its cash from the finance company as opposed to factoring which includes a more comprehensive sales ledger service.

When deciding which source of funds to use, companies have to consider factors such as availability, cost, risk, repayment burden if appropriate, and so on. Some of these factors are explored further in Chapter 13 which discusses the cost of capital.

Assets

A firm's possessions or assets are normally divided into two main categories – 'fixed' or long-term assets and 'current' or short-term assets. Sometimes other categories of asset appear in a particular firm's balance sheet. Examples are 'tangible assets' and 'investments' which comprise fixed assets. These various categories of asset and their bases of valuation under the historic cost convention are now explained in more detail.

Fixed assets

These are assets held in the business for use rather than for resale and can be regarded as long-term assets to be used for a number of years. Terms given to the four usual categories of tangible fixed assets are land and buildings, plant and machinery, motor vehicles and furniture and fittings.

Fixed assets are shown in the balance sheet at their original cost less the cumulative amount written off for depreciation. The main object of depreciation is to spread the original cost of the asset over its expected life so that the profit and loss account for any period bears a fair share of the cost of fixed assets. Consequently the value of fixed assets in the balance sheet may not exactly equal their saleable value at that time, particularly in times of rapid inflation. This problem is reserved for the next chapter and we are here concerned only with the original or historic cost of the asset.

Depreciation

In order to spread the cost of a fixed asset over its useful life we need to ascertain the original cost, the expected life and the residual or scrap value at the end of that life. Given these three pieces of information there is still more than one method which can be used to calculate the annual charge for depreciation.

The 'straight-line method' is the simplest and most common method used on most fixed assets, excluding cars. It calculates the annual depreciation charge by dividing the original cost, less any estimated residual value, by the estimated life of the asset. An example of the annual depreciation charge on this method is as follows:

$$\frac{\text{cost of machine £11,000 less scrap value £1,000}}{\text{estimated life 5 years}} = \frac{10,000}{5} = £2,000 \text{ p.a.}$$

Under this method the balance sheet value of the asset reduces by a constant amount each year.

A variation of this straight-line method is to calculate the life in hours rather than years, so expressing the depreciation charge as £X per hour. This machine-hour-rate method is often used in internal costings.

The other common method is primarily used for cars, other vehicles and some plant. It is called the 'reducing balance method' because depreciation is calculated on the reducing balance each year rather than on the original cost as with the straight-line method. This means that a much higher percentage rate is needed on the reducing balance method than the 20% applied to original cost, less scrap value, in the first method. This percentage rate (r) is derived from the formula:

$$r = 100 - \left(\sqrt[n]{\frac{\text{residual value}}{\text{original cost}}} \times 100 \right)$$

where n equals the estimated life in years. Using the previous example we can solve the equation:

$$r = 100 - \left(\sqrt[5]{\frac{\text{£1,000}}{\text{£11,000}}} \times 100 \right)$$
$$\therefore r = 38\%.$$

We can now use 38% as the rate of annual depreciation on the reducing balance, which will reduce the £11,000 cost to a written-down value of approximately £1,000 after five years. The calculations are set out in figure 4.1 and contrasted with the straight-line method.

Figure 4.1	Reducing balance method £	Straight-line method £
Original cost	11,000	11,000
First year depreciation (38%)	4,180	2,000
Balance sheet value – end Year 1	6,820	9,000
Second year depreciation (38%)	2,592	2,000
Balance sheet value – end Year 2	4,228	7,000
Third year depreciation (38%)	1,607	2,000
Balance sheet value – end Year 3	2,621	5,000
Fourth year depreciation (38%)	996	2,000
Balance sheet value – end Year 4	1,625	3,000
Fifth year depreciation (38%)	618	2,000
Balance sheet value – end Year 5	1,007	1,000

The argument advanced for adopting this method rather than the simpler straight-line method is that the annual charge for depreciation reduces each year as the annual maintenance cost can be expected to rise, one thereby tending to offset the other. An alternative to the reducing balance method is the 'sum-of-the-digits' method which also charges a diminishing amount of depreciation each year. This method applies a fraction where the numerator is the remaining life and the denominator the sum of all the years' digits. This fraction is applied to the cost less residual value as shown in figure 4.2.

Figure 4.2 Sum-of-the-digits method

	Fraction		Net cost		Annual depreciation	Written-down value
Year 1	5/15	×	£10,000	=	£3,333	£7,667
2	4/15	×	£10,000	=	£2,667	£5,000
3	3/15	×	£10,000	=	£2,000	£3,000
4	2/15	×	£10,000	=	£1,333	£1,667
5	1/15	×	£10,000	=	£667	£1,000
Totals	15/15				£10,000	

The sum-of-the-digits method is little used this side of the Atlantic but it has the advantage of a less steep fall in the depreciation charge each year if that is desired. Other less common methods of charging depreciation are based on interest calculations. The 'sinking fund' method literally invests a yearly sum outside the business, which together with profits will accumulate to the replacement cost of the asset at the end of its life. Another method, called the annual charge or annuity, writes off the cost of the asset and interest on the capital tied up in that asset. It can therefore be likened to a building society mortgage, the repayments on which comprise part capital and part interest on the capital outstanding each year.

Current assets

These include assets which are already cash or which are intended to be turned back into cash in the course of normal trading activity. They are short-term assets in the process of being sold to customers and being converted to cash again. There are three main types of current assets, namely stocks, debtors and cash itself, so we shall examine each in turn.

Stocks

It is possible to have up to three types of stock, depending on the nature of a business. The three categories are raw materials, work-in-progress and finished goods. A manufacturing firm will have all three kinds whereas a retail outlet will only have finished goods for resale. Service industries may also carry stocks. For example, an architect has considerable work-in-progress being the labour plus overhead costs of the drawings not yet charged to clients.

Stocks are valued on the basis of their cost, or realizable value if lower. Realizable value means their value to the trade not their sale value to a customer. This can be important for firms holding stocks of commodities, for example, tin, lead, cocoa whose prices can be volatile at times. Valuing these stocks at the year end may result in a loss if realizable value happens to be lower than cost at that particular moment. Metal merchants and confectionery manufacturers can see their profits affected either way by sharp changes in commodity prices.

The valuation of work-in-progress and finished goods may not be quite so straightforward as 'valuing at cost' suggests. In this context it is debatable what constitutes cost. Obviously the direct costs of labour and materials which went into making the product are part of the cost. So too is a share of the overhead costs of running the firm but this is the more difficult area. It can be argued that all production and administrative overheads should be charged to all products whether part or wholly finished. Selling and distribution overheads however should only apply to the goods sold and not by definition to the goods in stock. Fortunately some rules have been formulated by the accountancy profession and these are found in 'statement of standard accounting practice' (SSAP) No. 9.

The value of any stocks is also influenced by the pricing method used when issues from store occur. Stores issues can be priced on the basis of the purchase cost of the goods involved, but as this may vary over time various prices may have been paid for the total stock held. A decision has to be made between charging the issues on a 'last in first out' (LIFO) basis or a 'first in first out' (FIFO) basis. The latter is more common in the UK whilst LIFO is more common in the USA.

An alternative is to calculate a new average price every time a purchase is made and this represents a middle road approach. When firms use standard costing systems they usually hold materials in stock at the predetermined standard price. Any difference from this price is transferred to the profit and loss account at the time of purchase.

The choice of method will influence the profit made in any one year and the value of the stock remaining at the year end. Over a number of years, however, the total profit made will equate whichever method is used. The Inland Revenue may prefer some methods to others, but whichever basis is chosen it must be applied consistently from year to year.

Debtors

Debtors only arise where firms sell on credit, but as this is normal for all industries except retailing, then debtors are to be found in most balance sheets. Usually included in this heading are payments in advance as when, for example, rent and rates are paid for a period straddling two accounting years.

The basis for valuing debtors is to take the value of the invoices outstanding at the date of the balance sheet but to make a small adjustment to the total. Past experience will show that in most firms a small fraction of the customers' invoices never get paid in full. Usually this is because those customers go out of business unable to pay their debts, but it may also include unresolved disputes about the delivery or quality of the goods supplied.

Therefore firms make a small provision, based on past experience, of the amount which they should classify as doubtful debts. This provision is charged as an expense in the profit and loss account thus negating sales of that amount. During the year actual bad debts will arise so using up the provision. At the next year end the provision is restored to the required level in the light of the volume of trade and business conditions then prevailing.

Cash and bank balances

Included in this heading are cash floats, petty cash and receipts not yet banked. Firms will also usually have current and possibly deposit account balances which are also classified as cash. There are no valuation problems here.

Investments

Included in current assets it is not uncommon to see funds which have been temporarily invested until such time as the firm requires the money for investment within the business. Suitable short-term investments include government stocks or tax reserve certificates, provided the return is greater than that simply earned on bank deposits or lending to the money market. Investments that fluctuate in value are usually shown in the balance sheet at cost, with the market value shown alongside by way of a note.

When investments are of a long-term nature they are shown under a separate heading within fixed assets. Such investments include the cost of shares in subsidiary and related companies in addition to strategic holdings in other firms. These may be competitors, customers and suppliers or a potential takeover target for the future.

Goodwill, patents and trade marks

A firm is often worth more as a going concern than the total value of its assets. The difference between the value of its 'tangible' assets and its value as a going concern is called goodwill. Patents and trade marks are generally grouped with goodwill because of their close association. If the firm were to sell its trade mark, it would in effect be selling part of its goodwill. The accountant, however, only includes as assets items which have been bought. Therefore goodwill only appears in a balance sheet when it is bought, as when one firm buys another business as a g%ing concern and pays more for it than the total value of the individual assets.

Goodwill can change in value quite rapidly. The goodwill which has been bought for a large sum one year may be worth twice that figure or may have largely disappeared within a year or two in response to more or less efficient management. Therefore it is common practice to 'write off' goodwill out of profits as quickly as possible. Goodwill, if any, then appears in the balance sheet at cost less amounts written off up to that date.

Balance sheet sequence

The foregoing groups of assets are normally listed in the balance sheet in descending order of 'permanence' which might alternatively be described as ascending order of liquidity. In other words, the intangible asset of goodwill which the firm is least likely to sell is followed by tangible fixed assets, then investments, with current assets last of all. Within each category the same rules also apply, so that the sequence of tangible fixed assets runs: land and buildings, plant and machinery, fixtures and fittings, motor vehicles.

Self-check questions

1 Differentiate between ordinary and preference shares.
2 Differentiate between capital and revenue reserves.
3 Differentiate between long-term and current liabilities.
4 What is the written-down value of a machine costing £15,000 after three years, if a 20% reducing balance rate is applied?
5 Name the three possible types of stock.
6 What is a provision for bad debts?
7 Why is goodwill rarely seen in a company balance sheet?

5 Inflation accounting

Unfortunately inflation is like the poor – always with us. Economic historians can point to times past when the value of money actually increased but these have been short-lived. In the present inflationary era we need to be able to distinguish between the *apparent* profit of a business and its *real* profit after allowing for inflation.

This chapter explains the problems caused by inflation before explaining how accountants deal with them in accounting statements.

The problem of inflation

Inflation has been present in the UK, as in the world economy, throughout the whole postwar period. When the rate of inflation was at a mild rate of less than 5% per annum, accountants along with others largely ignored its existence when preparing the annual accounting statements of profit and loss account and balance sheet. Over a number of years, however, even a modest rate of inflation like 5% per annum has a dramatic effect on the value of the assets of a firm. Even more important is the effect on the replacement cost of such assets when they eventually wear out and have to be renewed.

For example, a firm buys fixed assets costing £2m and charges depreciation on their historic cost at £400,000 per annum for five years. Profits are fully distributed to shareholders each year so that no additional capital is retained from this source. Assuming inflation at 10% per annum the replacement cost of the fixed assets is £3,222,000 at the end of five years, but only £2m depreciation has been accumulated. Therefore £1,222,000 new capital may have to be raised just to continue in business. Even if the depreciation funds were invested each year outside the business a substantial deficit would still occur between these funds and the replacement cost of the fixed assets.

A number of basic problems are presented by inflation when preparing the annual accounting statements of profit and loss account and balance sheet. Profits are overstated when the costs of depreciation and stock consumed during the year are based on their original acquisition cost and not on their current replacement cost. The values of fixed assets and stock shown in the balance sheet are understated when based on their original cost. In turn this under-values the capital employed in the company. The combination of these factors means that the return on capital is considerably overstated as the following example illustrates:

£10m historic cost profit
(charging depreciation and stocks at original cost)

£40m capital employed
(basing asset values on original cost less depreciation)

$$= 25\% \text{ return on capital}$$

£9m current cost profit
(charging depreciation and stocks at replacement cost)

£45m capital employed
(basing asset values on replacement cost less depreciation)

$$= 20\% \text{ return on capital}$$

Another problem caused by inflation is that assets held in the form of money lose some of their value over time. Debtors and cash itself are cases in point. Conversely, firms gain by borrowing money and owing creditors for supplies because no allowance for inflation is made at the time repayment takes place. These gains and losses are excluded from the conventional profit and loss account.

If *real* profits are not measured there is the danger that firms will be too generous with wage increases, dividend payments and other benefits to the detriment of reinvestment. Many companies are paying dividends they have not really earned because they have not allowed for the extra costs of inflation in their profit and loss accounts. If inflation is ignored in the day-to-day running of the business, there is also the danger that selling prices may not reflect the up-to-date costs of stock and asset replacements. Hence insufficient cash will be generated to maintain the same trading level without recourse to more and more borrowing.

In the 1970s when the rate of inflation in the UK rose into double figures, and by the mid-1970s threatened to turn us into a banana republic, the professional accountancy bodies were involved in a long debate about how best to show the effects of inflation in accounting statements. One contentious point was whether to use general or specific price indices when revaluing stock or fixed assets. Another issue was whether to show the whole effects of inflation as falling on the firms' owners or whether to apportion it to different providers of capital. Some members of the profession preferred to ignore inflation and advocated continuing to provide statements based on the original value of transactions, i.e. historic cost accounting.

Current cost accounting

In March 1980 the accountancy profession published its 'statement of standard accountancy practice' No. 16 entitled *Current Cost Accounting*. This SSAP required listed companies and larger private companies to clarify the effects of inflation on both the profit earned in the year and on the value of assets held at the year end. This was achieved by the company producing supplementary statements to the historic cost profit and loss account and balance sheet. Although this SSAP is now not mandatory for reasons explained later, it is useful to examine the processes involved to gain a better insight into the effects of inflation.

Current cost profit and loss account

The supplementary profit and loss account statement contains four adjustments to the 'historic cost' profit to arrive at the 'current cost' profit attributable to the owners as figure 5.1 illustrates.

The historic cost profit of £1,000,000 is shown as being overstated when compared to the current cost operating profit of £400,000 which allows for the inflated costs of replacing fixed assets and stocks and giving more credit to customers. Some of these additional costs are offset by not having to recompense lenders of capital so that the current cost profit earned for the owners comes out at £640,000.

The way the first three adjustments are calculated largely makes use of index numbers supplied by the Central Statistical Office in a monthly publication called *Price Index Numbers for Current Cost Accounting*. In it the price movements of various assets and materials are recorded in detail for a variety of industries. In the event of a suitable index not being published a firm can construct its own in-house index.

Figure 5.1 Example of a current cost profit and loss account

			£000
Profit as in 'historic cost' profit and loss account			1,000
deduct (1) DEPRECIATION ADJUSTMENT being the extra cost of depreciation calculated on the replacement cost of assets instead of their original cost		200	
(2) COST OF SALES ADJUSTMENT being the extra cash needed to replace stocks at prices ruling at the time of sale...........................		300	
(3) MONETARY WORKING CAPITAL ADJUSTMENT being the additional cash needed to give credit to customers for the value of goods which have cost more to produce		100	600
= current cost operating profit..400			
add back (4) GEARING ADJUSTMENT being the proportion of the above adjustments (1), (2) and (3) not required to be borne by the owners if part of the firm's capital is borrowed (assumed 40% in this example)............................240			
= current cost profit earned for owners 640			

To illustrate the basic approach the depreciation adjustment is calculated from the following information:

A firm bought some fixed assets during 1979 at a cost of £2m and expected them to have a five-year life. Depreciation on a straight-line basis amounts to £400,000 per annum. The average price index for this type of asset was 120 in 1979 and 180 in 1983. The depreciation adjustment for 1983 gives the additional depreciation required to supplement the original £400,000 depreciation charged in the historic cost profit and loss account. In this example the extra depreciation amounts to £200,000 for 1983 and this figure appears in the supplementary current cost profit and loss account. The calculations are:

Total depreciation charge based on current cost £400,000 × $\frac{180}{120}$ =	£600,000
Depreciation already provided in historic cost profit and loss account	£400,000
Depreciation adjustment for 1983	£200,000

Current cost balance sheet

The supplementary balance sheet values all assets at their current replacement cost at the balance sheet date. When inflation increases the value of an asset in money terms, it might appear that the balance sheet will no longer balance. This is remedied by creating a special reserve called a 'current cost reserve' which is part of the shareholders' funds and effectively updates the value of the shareholders' investment in the business. If, for example, the value of fixed assets rose by £1m by the year end then this reserve will also be increased by £1m. This keeps intact the balance sheet equation that assets must always equal liabilities.

Let us take the example of a firm owning £1m assets financed totally by share capital. The financial position can be set out:

Balance sheet
Share capital £1,000,000 = Assets £1,000,000

Assume that because of inflation the assets increase in value by £50,000. The position now is:

	Balance sheet	
Share capital	£1,000,000	
Current cost reserve	£50,000	= Assets £1,050,000
	£1,050,000	

The differences between a current cost balance sheet and an historic cost one are limited to the valuation of assets and the current cost reserve. All assets are revalued to their replacement cost at the balance sheet date whilst debtors and cash remain unaffected. All liabilities are unaffected by inflation except for the current cost reserve which accumulates the asset revaluations and the four profit adjustments.

Reactions

SSAP 16 was introduced for a trial period of three years to be reviewed in 1983. Its use was extended until 1985 when it ceased to be mandatory due to lack of support from within and without the profession. Accountants found it an expensive and time-consuming task to produce the required data in another form. They also found a mixed response from intended users of the additional information either on the grounds of its complexity or disagreement with the rationale, and it is now applied by few firms.

There was hope that the Inland Revenue would accept the current cost procedures outlined in SSAP 16 as a basis for taxing real profits. They appear to have rejected this on the grounds of the subjectivity allowed to individual companies when choosing relevant price indices and asset lives.

It is doubtful if company managers, investors, employees and possibly even accountants understood all the ramifications of the current cost adjustments. The effects of inflation on pricing policy, working capital requirements, corporation tax assessments, dividend policy, and the cost of capital and wage claims are complex and not easily understood. The tendency was for companies, unions and the financial press to concentrate on the well-known but misleading figures and ignore the more accurate supplementary information.

In 1980 a leading firm of stockbrokers estimated that 40% of UK companies were paying dividends not covered by 'current cost earnings', i.e. excessive dividends were eroding the real capital base of these companies. With inflation down to around 5% by the mid-1980s this is no longer the case, especially as many companies pay less than half their profit out as dividends.

This chapter has concentrated on the effects of inflation on information contained in the annual accounting statements of the profit and loss account and balance sheet. It demonstrates how, if inflation is ignored, profits are overstated and assets are understated in terms of the current value of money.

Accountancy procedures used in the early 1980s to correct this, by producing supplementary statements, have been explained. These allow a more correct assessment of the return on capital, of the profits available for distribution as dividends, and of the book value of company shares.

Inflation has other effects on company finances. Questions as to what values to use when pricing, budgeting, setting standards and appraising investments are left until the relevant chapters containing these techniques.

Further reading

The Meaning of Company Accounts, W. Reid and D. R. Myddelton, Gower.
Accounting Under Inflationary Conditions, P. R. A. Kirkman, George Allen & Unwin.
'Statement of standard accounting practice' No. 16: *Current Cost Accounting*.

Self-check questions

1 What is the difference between an historic cost profit and a current cost profit?
2 What happens if a firm distributes all of its historic cost profit as dividends at a time of high inflation?
3 Name the four adjustments to historic cost profit that appear in a current cost profit and loss account.
4 If an asset is revalued how does a balance sheet still balance?

6 Performance ratios

Previous chapters have examined the two most important financial statements of profit and loss account and balance sheet. The trading performance of a company for a period of time is measured in the profit and loss account by deducting running costs from sales income. A balance sheet sets out the financial position of the company at a particular point in time, namely, the end of the accounting period. It lists the assets still owned by the company at that date matched by an equal list of the sources of finance.

A person experienced in reading company accounts can get some insight into a company's affairs by examining these financial statements. Changes in some of the key figures are apparent from the adjacent figure for the previous year, but such an approach can be misleading. Consider a company whose profit increased by 10% over the previous year. This might appear to be a good performance until one considers either a 15% rate of inflation or the extra 20% of capital employed to earn that extra profit. Experienced and inexperienced readers of accounts will benefit from a more methodical analysis of the figures.

The main analytical approach is to examine the relationship of pairs of figures extracted from the accounts. A pair may be taken from the same statement or one figure from each of the profit and loss account and balance sheet. When brought together the two figures are called ratios, although this term is not always used in the normal sense of the word. Some of the ratios are meaningful in themselves but their value mainly lies in their comparison with the equivalent ratio last year, a target ratio or a competitor's ratio.

All too frequently one sees television or newspaper reporting that some leading company made £Xm profit last year. As a sum of money the figures sound very large and more naïve audiences might be tempted to think of excessive prices being charged. Such reporting is almost meaningless without reference to last year's figure, the size of the company's sales or amount of capital employed. In other words the absolute value of profit is not as meaningful as the 'return on capital' or 'profit margin' on sales.

Profitability

Most of the main ratios are concerned with aspects of profitability and, like any investment, the key ratio is the return on the investment. We calculate this by expressing profit as a percentage of capital. This is influenced by two further ratios comprising the profit margin (profit as a percentage of sales) and the rate of asset turnover (sales divided by capital). Using sample figures when profit is £1m, sales are £10m and capital is £5m then:

$$\frac{profit\ \pounds1m}{capital\ (assets)\ \pounds5m}\% = \frac{profit\ \pounds1m}{sales\ \pounds10m}\% \times \frac{sales\ \pounds10m}{capital\ (assets)\ \pounds5m}$$

$$\begin{array}{ccccc} 20\% & & 10\% & & 2\ times \\ return\ on\ capital & = & profit\ margin & \times & rate\ of\ asset\ turnover \end{array}$$

The return on capital may vary from one industry to another but wider variations may be found in their profit margin and rates of asset turnover. Figure 6.1 shows various ways in which, say, a 20% return on capital could be achieved in different industries:

Figure 6.1 Sample performance ratios

Industry	return on capital	=	profit margin	×	rate of asset turnover
Construction	20%	=	4%	×	5 times
Food retailing	20%	=	2%	×	10 times
Heavy engineering	20%	=	10%	×	2 times

Profit margins in food retailing may be only 2–3% but this is offset by a very high rate of asset turnover. In more capital-intensive industries with a long production cycle the low rate of asset turnover is compensated for by a high profit margin.

These three key ratios are only the starting point from which a number of subsidiary ratios can be calculated relating running costs or assets to sales. Figure 6.2 shows this approach in diagrammatic form.

The precise definition and meaning of the most important ratios are now given.

Figure 6.2 Diagram of key performance ratios

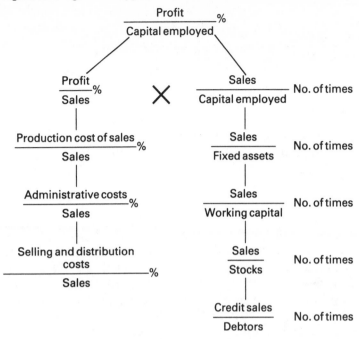

Profit/capital

This ratio is usually expressed as a percentage in the way we might think of the return on any financial investment. Both profit and capital may be defined in different ways, the choice of which depends on the use to which the ratio is put. Looked at from the owners' viewpoint, their concern is with the profit earned for them relative to the amount of funds they have invested in the business. The relevant profit here is after interest, tax and preference dividends have been deducted. This is expressed as a percentage of ordinary shareholders' funds comprising both share capital and reserves:

$$\text{return on shareholders' funds} = \frac{\text{profit after tax, interest and pref. divds}}{\text{ordinary shareholders' funds}}\%$$

The above ratio will be influenced not only by the trading performance but by the size of tax allowances and the mix of owners' and borrowed capital used by that particular company. A wider view of company performance can be taken by expressing profit before

67

interest, tax and preference dividends as a percentage of the total capital employed, irrespective of whether the capital is borrowed or provided by the owners. This states:

$$\text{return on capital} = \frac{\text{profit before tax, interest and dividends}}{\text{total capital employed}}\%$$

Profit/sales

In effect this ratio measures the net profit margin as a percentage but it is common practice in many industries to scrutinize the gross margin in addition.

$$\text{profit margin} = \frac{\text{net profit before tax, interest and dividends}}{\text{sales}}\%$$

It is usual to take the profit before tax, interest and dividends as all three are subject to variations which have nothing to do with the basic trading performance. We are really saying that profit margins are determined by operating costs and selling prices rather than the capital mix or effective tax rate at any point of time. An extension of this ratio is to express every profit and loss item as a percentage of sales. Here is an example with hypothetical figures:

	%
Direct labour/sales	23
Direct material/sales	25
Production overheads/sales	14
Administration overheads/sales	15
Selling and distribution overheads/sales	13
Profit/sales	10
	100%

As previously stated the absolute value of these ratios has little meaning. Ratios are like fingerprints in detective work. They point us in a direction that appears to merit further investigation when they compare adversely with previous experience, targets or competitors' ratios.

Sales/capital (or assets)

This ratio is usually expressed as a rate of turnover. For example, if capital is £2m when sales are £4m we say capital employed was turned over twice during the year. Another way of expressing this would be to say £0.50 assets were needed per £1 of sales.

$$\text{turnover of capital} = \frac{\text{sales £4m}}{\text{capital employed £2m}} = 2 \text{ times}$$

Capital employed is the total amount of permanent and long-term capital excluding current liabilities. Subsidiary ratios may relate groups of assets, or any individual asset, to sales. If, say, sales are £4m and fixed assets £0.8m then:

$$\text{rate of fixed asset turnover} = \frac{\text{sales £4m}}{\text{fixed assets £0.8m}} = 5 \text{ times}$$

An alternative way of expressing this is to say £1 of fixed assets generated £5 of sales in the year. A similar calculation could be performed on working capital to identify the velocity of circulation of the same money being used over and over again.

To illustrate if sales are £4m and working capital is £1.2m then the rate of turnover of working capital is:

$$\text{rate of turnover of working capital} = \frac{\text{sales £4m}}{\text{working capital £1.2m}} = 3 \cdot 3 \text{ times}$$

When individual current assets are related to sales, however, it is common practice to invert the ratio and multiply by 52 weeks. Applied to debtors the ratio debtors/sales × 52 tells us the number of weeks' credit being taken by customers. Ignoring seasonal fluctuations in sales, when annual sales are £4m and debtors are £0.5m then:

$$\text{credit period taken} = \frac{\text{debtors £0.5m}}{\text{sales £4m}} \times 52 \text{ weeks} = 6\tfrac{1}{2} \text{weeks}$$

Similarly the ratio stock/cost of sales × 52 tells us the number of weeks' stock being carried and the ratio creditors/purchases × 52 denotes the period of credit taken from suppliers.

Liquidity

Previous ratios have examined the performance of a company from the viewpoint of efficiency, both in the control of costs and in the use of its assets. In order to survive, companies must also watch their liquidity position, by which is meant keeping enough short-term assets to pay short-term debts. Companies go out of business compulsorily when they fail to pay money due to employees, bankers or suppliers. There are two main ratios used to examine the liquidity position of a company, namely the liquidity ratio and the current ratio.

Liquidity ratio

This is sometimes called the acid test ratio because it is the one that really matters. It takes the form of liquid assets : current liabilities where a 1:1 ratio means a company has sufficient cash or near cash to pay its immediate debts. Liquid assets are defined here as all the current assets excluding stocks which cannot quickly be converted into cash. In effect liquid assets are debtors, cash and any short-term investments like bank deposits or government securities. Using the figures in Appendix 2 the liquidity ratio can be calculated as follows, showing ample liquid resources at that moment in time:

$$\text{liquidity ratio} = \frac{\text{liquid assets} \quad £38,000}{\text{current liabilities} \quad £30,000} = 1.3:1$$

A company can survive with a liquidity ratio of less than 1:1 if it has unused bank overdraft facilities. Any existing bank overdraft is classified as a current liability but if not called in, it should not really count as a short-term debt. Funding an overdraft with a longer-term loan would also transform an adverse liquidity ratio.

In some industries it is not unusual for stocks and work-in-progress to be turned into cash before all creditors are due for payment. Building construction and food retailing are cases in point where seemingly adverse liquidity ratios pose no threat to the company.

Current ratio

The other test of a company's liquidity includes stocks and work-in-progress on the grounds that stocks eventually turn into debtors and then into cash itself. It is calculated by relating all current assets to current liabilities. A norm of 2:1 is regarded as satisfactory in most industries but this is a somewhat arbitrary figure and it may be a better guide to look at the norm for each particular industry. The above points about bank overdrafts also apply as do the ability of some firms to turn stocks into cash more quickly than most.

Again using the figures in Appendix 2 the current ratio is:

$$\text{current ratio} = \frac{\text{current assets} \quad £73,000}{\text{current liabilities} \quad £30,000} = 2.4:1$$

indicating this company has more than sufficient short-term assets to meet its short-term debts.

Debt capacity

The distinguishing features of borrowed capital as opposed to owners' capital are that borrowings must be serviced by interest payments and repaid either in instalments or at the end of a period of years. There is no such legal obligation to pay dividends to owners, nor is share capital repayable. From a liquidity point of view too much debt is risky, as the higher the proportion of capital raised by loans the higher the proportion of profit going as interest. A judicious amount of borrowed capital can be beneficial to the owners and this aspect is discussed in Chapter 13 under the heading of 'capital gearing'. For the moment let us examine the ratios concerned with measuring the amount of debt a company can assume.

Debt ratio

The proportion of debt to total assets expressed as a percentage is used to quantify the amount of debt owed by a firm. In effect, this ratio measures the proportion of assets owned by a company which is owed to creditors of various kinds. In this context, debt includes all loans, overdrafts, trade creditors, tax and other liabilities. The higher the percentage, the less willing creditors will be to extend further credit.

Borrowing ratio

This measures the proportion of total borrowing, including long-term loans and bank overdrafts, to either total capital employed or shareholders' funds. For example, when total borrowings are £4m and shareholders' funds are £16m then total capital employed equals £20m. Borrowings therefore represent 25% of shareholders' funds or 20% of total capital employed. This level of borrowing would not be regarded as excessive but the volatility of profits in the past must be considered before making a final judgement.

Income gearing

A measure of the proportion of profit taken up by interest payments can be gained by expressing the annual interest payment as a percentage of the annual profit before interest, tax and dividend payments. The smaller the percentage then the less vulnerable the company will be to any setback in profits or rise in interest rates on variable loans. The larger the percentage then the more risk that level of borrowing represents to the company. For example when annual interest is £70,000 and profit £100,000 then:

$$\text{income gearing} = \frac{\text{interest} \quad £70,000}{\text{profit} \quad £100,000} = 70\%$$

which figure leaves the company very vulnerable to any profits setback.

An alternative way of calculating this risk would be to calculate the interest cover being profit divided by interest which equals 1.4 times in this example. One must also look for peculiarities in any one industry. Property development is heavily dependent on borrowed capital and any dramatic change in market conditions for letting can pose severe problems for the companies concerned. Memories of the property boom and collapse which triggered off the secondary banking crisis of the 1970s still linger on.

Interfirm comparisons

Mention was made earlier that ratios can be used to compare aspects of one company's performance with competitors. It is possible to conduct such an exercise by using the information in the published annual accounts of similar firms. This information can be requested from the company or more usually extracted from a data base like Extel which is found in many large libraries. Alternatively a search can be instigated at Companies House but this may prove expensive when a number of companies are involved.

Some firms use an organization called the Centre for Interfirm Comparisons and participate in a study of their industry. Financial information, including detailed costs, is submitted in confidence and comparative ratios produced. Data must be adjusted to a common basis for all firms so that, for instance, a firm which leased all its assets adjusts its costs and assets to align with other firms who own their assets.

Limitations

It should not be thought that performance ratios are a panacea for all ills. They are a relatively crude diagnostic tool which can help managers and investors identify the strengths and weaknesses of a company. They identify the areas to examine in more depth but suffer from the limitations of the financial statements from which they are prepared. In particular, care must be taken when deciding whether to use inflation-adjusted data to calculate ratios.

Further reading

Management Accounting, Graham Mott, Pan.
The Meaning of Company Accounts, W. Reid and D. R. Myddelton, Gower.
How to Use Management Ratios, C. A. Westwick, Gower.

Self-check questions

1 What is an accounting ratio?
2 Complete the following equation:

return on capital = profit margin × ....

3 Is there an ideal value for each ratio? If not, how are ratios used?
4 Which ratio would you use to examine whether a company was short of cash if you knew it could not borrow any more money?
5 Which company is more vulnerable? Company A which pays annual interest of £50,000 and makes a profit of £100,000 or Company B which pays £150,000 interest and makes £500,000 profit?

7 Statement of sources and applications of funds

Readers of annual reports need some training to understand profit and loss accounts and balance sheets. They may be heartened by this further statement whose title accurately describes its contents. A sources and applications of funds statement summarizes exactly where cash came from and how it was spent during the year. As such it includes cash transactions concerning both the profit and loss account and balance sheet as this simplified diagram shows:

Figure 7.1

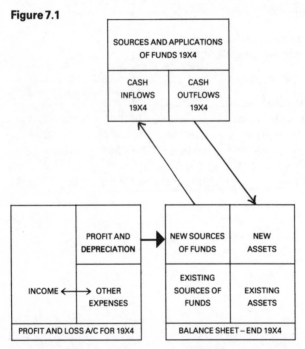

The prime source of cash for any company should be the sale of goods and services for more than their cost to produce. In other words profit is a most important source of cash. When examining the profit and loss account we saw that depreciation was included in the list of expenses. As it is a *notional* transaction and not a real payment of cash, we add it back to profit as though it had never been deducted in the first place.

Another internal source of cash may be the sale of scrap or redundant assets. Together with profit and depreciation these form the sources of cash generated from trading operations.

Next come the external sources of cash by way of new capital raised during the year. This may take the form of a new issue of shares or a loan or debenture for a number of years. These internal and external sources of cash now make up the total funds received during the year.

From this total is first deducted the applications of cash going outside the business. These will include tax payments but because of the normal time allowed the tax paid will mainly relate to the previous year's profit rather than the current year. Similarly with dividends, as the final dividend of one year is never actually declared and paid in cash until the next accounting year. This is why these items are usual constituents of current liabilities at the year end. Other payments of cash may be the purchase of fixed assets and investments. If the total of these tax, dividend and new asset payments are deducted from total sources of funds we are left with the change in total working capital. Describing profit as a source of cash may not seem strictly correct when the profit and loss account includes some credit transactions not yet completed in cash terms. We allow for these uncompleted cash transactions by showing the change in debtors and creditors during the year as part of the change in working capital. The other items in this section are the change in stock levels and the movement of liquid funds comprising cash, bank balance or overdraft.

A typical statement in SSAP 10 format is shown in figure 7.2.

Figure 7.2 Statement of sources and applications of funds

		£000
Sources of funds		
Profit before tax		105
add back Depreciation		15
Total generated from trading operations		120
Other sources:		
Issue of new shares		45
Loan		15
Total sources of funds		180
Applications of funds		
Payment of tax	40	
Payment of dividend	35	
Purchase of fixed assets	50	125
Increase in working capital		55
Increase in stocks	47	
Increase in debtors	30	
Increase in creditors	(27)	
Increase in liquid funds	5	55

Purpose of the statement

A statement of sources and applications of funds has two main purposes – to show how a company financed itself during the year and also to identify where the money was spent. The sources section of the statement splits into two parts. The funds generated from trading operations demonstrates how self-reliant the company is in generating all the cash it needs internally, as opposed to going outside for new capital. In figure 7.2 we can see that the company generated two-thirds of the cash required internally and had to go outside to raise the remaining one-third. Many companies may be totally self-financing but this must be examined in the context of whether the firm is stagnant or expanding in real terms.

The applications part of the statement shows where the funds were spent. Some money goes to make tax and dividend payments mainly in respect of the previous year. The remaining cash either goes to pay for the acquisition of fixed assets and investments or it goes into working capital. If firms are buying more fixed assets than the depreciation provision this may point to an expansion, particularly if depreciation has been calculated on the current cost of assets. If working capital has increased this may point to expansion, the effects of inflation, or simply loose control of stocks and debtors. Conversely a fall in working capital may be caused by trading at a loss, a contraction in the volume of business, better control of stocks and debtors or an impending liquidity problem.

Shareholders, analysts and management can all usefully study this statement particularly if read in conjunction with the directors' and chairman's reports on the state of the business.

Preparation of the statement

If we refer back to figure 7.1 we can see that the balance sheet is the key statement providing information on the sources and applications of funds. We can examine the changes which have taken place between the opening and closing balance sheets of the year under review. These changes can be identified as either a source of cash or a use of cash according to the nature of the items. In most cases it will be obvious whether it is a source or use but logic can be tested by following these rules:

- If an item on the *sources* side of the balance sheet (e.g. share capital, loans or creditors) has *increased* during the year then this obviously represents an inflow of funds.
- Conversely, if an item on the sources side has *decreased* then this is an *outflow* (e.g. a loan repayment).
- In the case of the *assets* an *increase* represents an *outflow* of funds (e.g. the purchase of a new piece of plant or extra stock).
- Conversely a *decrease* in assets must represent an *inflow* of funds, possibly from the sale of the asset.

The only exceptions to this procedure of identifying the change in balance sheet items occur with tax and dividends shown as current liabilities. These are appropriations of profit for the year so we add back the whole of the latest outstanding amounts to retained profit, thus arriving at the profit before tax and dividend payments. The amounts of tax and dividends outstanding at the previous year end will have been paid during the later year being reviewed and are therefore shown as applications of funds. This procedure is followed in figure 7.3.

Having identified the changes in balance sheet items as either sources or uses of cash, these can now be set out in the sources and applications of funds statement as in figure 7.4.

In practice this procedure forms a very good starting point, but the statement may have to be modified in the light of further

Figure 7.3 Identification of sources and uses of cash in Year 2

Balance sheet £000	Year 1	Year 2	Source	Use
Premises at cost	100	130		30
Plant and machinery at cost	156	168		12
less Depreciation	54	70	16	
Stocks and wok-in-progress	58	101		43
Debtors	68	94		26
Cash	10	—	10†	
Total as 338	423			
Issued share capital	120	140	20	
Reserves – Share premium A/C	20	40	20	
– Retained profits	85	103	18*	
12% loan	40	60	20	
Creditors	48	52	4	
Provision for current tax	9	12	12*	9
Proposed dividend	16	10	10*	16
Bank overdraft	—	6	6†	—
Total capital	338	423		
			136	136

Note: Items marked * make up profit before charging tax and dividends.
Items marked † make up change in net liquid funds.

Figure 7.4 Sources and applications of funds for Year 2

Sources of funds		£000
Profit before tax and dividends (18+12+10)		40
add back Depreciation		16
Total generated from trading operations		56
Other sources:		
Issue of shares for cash	40	
New loan	20	60
Total sources of funds		116
Applications of funds		
Payment of tax	9	
Payment of dividend	16	
Purchase of fixed assets	42	67
Increase in working capital		49
Increase in stocks and work-in-progress	43	
Increase in debtors	26	
Increase in creditors	(4)	
Decrease in net liquid funds (10+6)	(16)	49

information available in the profit and loss account or the notes to the accounts. For example, an interim dividend may already have been paid. This would increase the profit figure in the sources of funds and the payment of dividend in the applications of funds. Another possibility is that an increase in fixed assets resulted from a revaluation rather than new purchases. Such increases are not movements of cash and have to be eliminated from the changes in fixed assets and reserves where the revaluation is recorded.

Notwithstanding these more technical points it is possible to get a good view of the adequacy of a company's cash flow from the preparation and study of a sources and applications of funds statement.

Further reading

The Meaning of Company Accounts, W. Reid and D. R. Myddelton, Gower.
'Statement of standard accounting practice' No. 10.

Self-check questions

1 Why do firms produce a statement of sources and applications of funds in addition to a profit and loss account and balance sheet?
2 Prepare a statement of sources and applications of funds for Year 2 from the following balance sheet information (see overleaf):

		Balance sheets		
		Year 1		Year 2
		£		£
Fixed assets				
Land and buildings at cost		50,000		55,000
Plant and machinery at cost	65,000		100,000	
less Depreciation	43,000	22,000	55,000	45,000
		72,000		100,000
Current assets				
Stocks and work-in-progress	58,000		66,000	
Debtors	29,500		42,000	
Cash	10,000	97,500	12,000	120,000
less Current liabilities				
Creditors	25,000		32,000	
Taxation	11,000		17,000	
Proposed dividend	7,500	(43,500)	10,000	(59,000)
		£126,000		£161,000
Financed by				
Share capital		90,000		90,000
Reserves		25,000		40,000
Loans		11,000		31,000
		£126,000		£161,000

8 Value added

The gross domestic product (GDP) of any country is the value of the wealth created in that country during a period of time, usually measured over a year.

This wealth is the value of the goods and services produced by measurable economic activity – in other words the money value of the output of firms of all sizes in all industries. There are some problems posed for the government statisticians when they tackle this exercise. The most obvious one is how to avoid double counting the same output when it is passed from one firm to another and one industry to another.

The answer lies in calculating the size of output on a value added basis. Take for example the coal industry. Coal is used to generate electricity which is used to produce steel which in turn is used to manufacture cars. If we take the total value of coal, electricity, steel and cars produced in the UK in a year we would be counting the value of some coal four times and not just once. But if we deduct the value of all the bought-in goods and services from the sales of each industry we are left with the value added by that industry alone. This avoids all double counting. Therefore:

| VALUE ADDED | = | SALES | − | BOUGHT-IN GOODS AND SERVICES |

Just as we can measure the wealth created by a country or an industry so we can for one company. The wealth created by any business is the value of its sales less the cost of all the bought-in goods and services (which is wealth created by other firms). All firms are creators of wealth. They buy in raw materials and services which they then convert or process into a product or service which in turn they sell to their own customers. The difference between the final sales value and the original bought-in materials and services is the value added by that firm. It is this wealth which a company has available for distribution to the four interested parties – employees, government, providers of capital and the company itself.

We can think of a firm as a kind of partnership between these four parties. Employees bring their various skills whilst the government provides the environment in which firms and employees more easily prosper from the various services provided. Shareholders and loan providers allow their capital to be used to finance the production process whilst the firm brings together all the assets needed to carry out its economic function. It is these four partners who always share in the wealth created by themselves, although the shares are by no means equal. A typical value added statement for a firm appears in figure 8.1 but it should be remembered that the four-way split differs from firm to firm and industry to industry.

Figure 8.1 Typical value added statement

	£000
Sales	230
less Bought-in goods and services	130
Value added	100

This was distributed as follows:		
To employees – as wages, salaries, pension and National Insurance contributions	70	
To government – as taxes on profits	8	
To providers of capital – as interest on loans and dividends to shareholders	10	
To reinvestment – as depreciation and retained profits to finance replacement assets	12	100

The principles on which a value added statement is prepared are the same as for a profit and loss account. The conventions of realization and accrual are followed, as is the concept of matching 'cost of sales' with sales in the same accounting period. Therefore, any increase in stocks of work-in-progress and finished goods is not counted as part of wealth created in this period because the sale has not yet taken place. Conversely, a decrease in such stocks counts as wealth created in this period. Government statisticians, however, do take these stock changes into account when calculating the total value of national output. Companies likewise would also have to take these stock changes into account when basing incentive payments on value added.

Value added statements and profit and loss accounts are both prepared from the same financial data. Their difference lies in the presentation and orientation of the contents. A profit and loss account gives a narrow 'shareholder-centred' view of company performance, unashamedly so, because this is the design concept. The very word 'profit' does have an emotive and political undertone when viewed by parties other than shareholders. A value added statement, however, concentrates on wealth creation rather than profit and shows its distribution to all four parties, not just one, who have contributed. We can see both the similarities and the differences if we examine the two statements, both of which are prepared from the same basic data as in figure 8.2.

Figure 8.2 Comparison of profit and loss account with value added statement

Part (i) Profit and loss account for year 198X

		£000
Sales		1,000
less Materials used*	300	
Services purchased*	130	
Wages and salaries	350	
Depreciation	90	
Interest on loan	50	920
Profit before tax		80
Corporation tax on profit		30
Profit after tax		50
Dividends		30
Retained profit		20

Part (ii) Value added statement for 198X

		£000
Sales		1,000
less Bought-in materials and services*		430
Value added		570
This was distributed as follows:		
To employees – wages, salaries, pensions and NI	350	
To government – corporation tax on profit	30	
To providers of capital – dividends and interest	80	
To reinvestment – depreciation and retained profits ploughed back	110	570

Not all companies are producing value added statements as an integral part of their annual report, although the Corporate Report (1975) recommended that practice. One company which does produce a very readable statement is International Paints and an example of their approach is shown in figure 8.3.

In addition to the absolute values, the percentage share of value added going to each of the four parties is shown. This discloses a

**Figure 8.3 International Paints Statement of value added
year ended 31 March 1980**

		1980		1979
		£000		£000
Sales		239,548		217,267
less Bought-in materials and services		165,220		146,475
Value added by manufacturing and trading		74,328		70,792
Disposal of total value added:	%	£000	%	£000
Employees – wages, pensions and social security contributions	71	52,819	71	50,609
Taxation	7	5,412	9	6,474
Providers of capital				
Net interest		(1,273)		(711)
Minority shareholders in subsidiaries		1,700		1,346
Dividends to shareholders		2,243		1,926
	4	2,670	4	2,561
Reinvestment in the business				
Depreciation		2,758		2,518
Retained profit		10,669		8,630
	18	13,427	16	11,148
	100	74,328	100	70,792

very similar distribution of wealth in the two years mentioned. The fall in the share going to government probably results from tax allowances on the increased reinvestment in the business.

There are no fixed percentage shares of value added applicable to all companies. In a capital-intensive industry, the share of wealth going to labour should be smaller to allow for the servicing of large amounts of capital and a high level of reinvestment to replace worn-out plant. Conversely in a labour- or material-intensive industry the proportion of value added going to labour will be higher because the amount of capital to be serviced and the replacement investment are not so large.

It can be argued that in some firms the proportion of wealth going to one party has been too large resulting in too small a distribution elsewhere. The classic trade-off is between labour and capital reinvestment. Some financial experts have commented that in many of our declining industries, like vehicles, the level of reinvestment has been much too low to keep us competitive internationally. Others have pointed to our poor productivity which results in low value added, low reinvestment and an apparently high distribution of wealth to labour. This debate lies at the heart of how we are to improve our economic performance as a nation.

Uses of value added

There are two main uses to which value added statements can be put. A shareholder reading the statement can note the trend of distributions to himself, to the labour force and to reinvestment for growth. Any tendency to an increased labour share at the expense of reinvestment may lead him to reconsider his continued shareholding. Trades union officials and employees will find the value added statement more helpful to financially untrained minds than the profit and loss account. The size of value added puts an absolute maximum on employee remuneration even if one could ignore the legal claims for interest and tax. Employees are shown to be the recipients of the lion's share of wealth in every company and the debate on conflicting claims is more easily conducted using the value added statement. Perhaps more emphasis can be placed on increasing the size of the cake (value added) than on squabbling about the size of the four slices which in reality boils down to three or even only two.

The other main use of the value added concept is in measuring performance. Chapter 6 introduced the idea of using ratios to measure aspects of cost control and asset utilization aimed at improving the return on capital. In a similar way we can examine the trend of value added per worker or £ wages per £ value added to monitor labour productivity. Likewise we can appraise capital productivity via the ratio £ value added per £ capital employed. Comparisons of these ratios between similar firms can only stimulate a more informed debate on efficiency and productivity.

Consideration should also be given as to whether the value added statement is produced on an historic or current cost basis. The latter would seem more appropriate because only after allowing for the cost of sales, depreciation and monetary working capital adjustments can we talk about the real wealth created.

85

Employee reports

This topic is introduced here because of its affinity to the value added statement, which is often used to communicate basic financial information to employees in place of the profit and loss account. Most employees (and personal shareholders for that matter) find the annual accounts totally confusing and, increasingly, firms prepare a short salient financial report just for their employees' consumption. The cornerstone of this report is usually a value added approach, describing the wealth created in the year and how it has been distributed.

Sometimes an abbreviated profit and loss account is given but it is perhaps confusing to present both. Balance sheets are rarely given except in a highly summarized manner. The whole purpose of employee reporting is to communicate a few key facts on company performance which can be readily understood, rather than a morass of accounting detail which can thoroughly confuse the untrained reader.

Further reading

Added Value – The Key to Prosperity, E. G. Wood, Business Books.

Self-check questions

1 Define value added.
2 A value added statement is based on the same concepts, and uses the same information, as which statement?
3 How might a firm use the value added to measure changes in productivity and efficiency?
4 Name the four parties to whom value added is distributed.
5 Even when firms do not include a value added statement in their annual reports they may distribute one to which party?

Part 2
Management accounting

The financial statements found in the annual accounts are used by top management and external parties interested in the performance and financial position of the global enterprise. Functional managers within the firm will not find these financial statements of much help in the day-to-day running and management of resources under their control. Their need is for much more detailed information to allow them to price realistically and to plan and control future activities. Very many decisions which managers take are based on financial information. Knowing what information to ask for and how to use it is an essential requirement for any businessman. The second part of this book is concerned with just these techniques which assist managers in their jobs.

9 Product costing

All costs incurred by a business can be easily grouped under three main headings. Materials are commodities supplied to the firm and relevant information comes from the invoice, or stores requisition if issued from stock. Labour embraces wages, salaries and other remuneration paid to employees, details of which are entered on timecards or timesheets. Services are the third group and this covers all costs except labour and materials, but includes rent, rates, electricity and depreciation. The services provided by other firms are charged on an invoice. There are therefore three elements making up total cost.

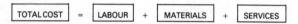

Information about these elements comes from the originating or prime documents. Such invoices, requisitions and timecards are given a code number describing all aspects of the cost as explained in Chapter 1. This allows a firm to input information into computer systems as a series of numbers including the value of the transaction.

Unfortunately, when calculating the cost of a product a further subdivision of costs has to be made. Certain costs can be readily identified with a particular job, product or process. Materials which literally form part of the product and productive labour are both good examples of these 'direct' or 'prime' costs. Other materials, like stationery, salaries of non-productive staff and most services cannot readily be identified with particular products and are therefore called 'indirect' or 'overhead' costs. In many firms these overhead costs amount to more than the prime costs. They are an essential expense and the term non-productive is used only in the sense of not directly producing the product for the customer.

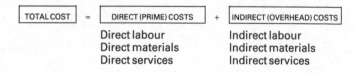

The total cost of any product comprises the direct costs plus a share, or apportionment, of the overheads. Direct costs can be cost coded to the particular job, product or service provided for the customer. Overhead or indirect costs, by definition, cannot be charged directly to one particular product. We therefore need to establish some mechanism by which we can charge a small part of the total overheads to each unit of a firm's output.

In a small firm, the view is taken that most overheads are related to the passing of time. Rent, rates, depreciation, supervision, office salaries and heating can be viewed as time-based costs. The products or services sold to customers take a certain time to make or provide, for which time the labour force is paid a proportionate sum of money. Linking these two aspects of time, small firms usually charge out overheads to products pro rata to the cost of direct labour going into the product.

Example

Mott Engineering Ltd estimate that their overheads for the next year will amount to £100,000 whilst direct labour costs are expected to be £80,000. Assuming the two estimated figures turn out to be correct, this company will recover all its overhead costs if it charges £1.25 overheads for every £1 direct labour charged to a product. In other words the overhead recovery rate is 125% of the direct labour cost:

$$\frac{£100,000}{£80,000} \times \frac{100}{1}\% = 125\%$$

These advance estimates may not turn out as expected. At the end of each quarter the overhead recovery rate should be recalculated in the light of up-to-date costs of both direct labour and overheads. This is necessary because trading conditions may have resulted in a changed labour force or unforeseen cost increases. Either of these factors could lead to an under- (or over-) recovery of overheads.

Most large firms do not use one global recovery rate for all overheads. Where diverse products are made with varying production processes the use of one global overhead recovery rate may result in some overheads being charged to products unfairly, and insufficient overheads being apportioned to others. Take for example the simplified case of a two-product firm in which one of the products requires the lengthy use of sophisticated electronic equipment in a test department. It is patently unfair to charge the costs of running the test department to both products. This would lead to incorrect total costs with possible repercussions on production and pricing decisions. What is needed, therefore, is a flexible method of channelling overheads from service departments to production departments and eventually to products.

Service departments are those non-producing departments which provide essential services to other departments and include such diverse functions as stores, maintenance and canteens. All the running costs of these service departments are overheads. Production departments also have their own overhead costs in the form of

Figure 9.1 Product costing procedure

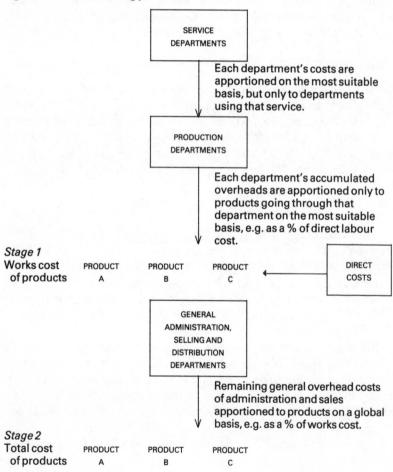

supervisory salaries and the cost of heating, lighting and cleaning. Having accumulated all production and service overheads in production departments, these are now apportioned only to products going through a particular department. This ensures products cannot be unfairly charged with services from which they have not benefited as in the example of Mott Engineering Ltd. At this stage the total production cost comprises the direct costs specifically charged together with an apportionment of overheads from relevant production and service departments. There remains the general administrative and selling expenses which are usually apportioned to products on a pro rata basis to works cost so arriving at the total cost of the product. This whole procedure is outlined in figure 9.1.

Bases of overhead apportionment

When apportioning service department costs to user departments the most suitable basis is used in each case. Service departments give service not only to production departments but also to other service departments. This requires a repetitive procedure sometimes, as further apportionments come in from other service departments after the initial apportionment has been made. In a large organization, where many services are involved, this results in a wide variety of apportionment bases being used. The following list gives some of the more common services and a suggested basis for overhead apportionment:

Service	Apportionment basis
Power	User department (if metered)
Heating, lighting, rent and rates	Floor area
Storekeeping	Value or number of items issued
Cleaning	Floor area or specific labour cost
Canteen	Number of employees
Maintenance	User department
Depreciation of machinery	Value of machinery used
National insurance, pension contributions	Wages cost
Employer's liability insurance	Wages cost
Training	Number of employees

Full cost pricing

The total cost of a product comprises its direct costs plus an apportionment of overheads. This is sometimes called absorption costing as products absorb all the overheads. Having arrived at the full, or total, cost of a product it can be used as a basis for fixing prices. It must be stressed that not all firms price in this way. Sometimes prices are fixed by a market leader or what the competition generally is charging. Customers also have a say in fixing prices as they may be unwilling to purchase, or seek alternative products, when prices are too high.

Notwithstanding these marketing aspects of pricing, many firms price some or all of their products on the basis of total (full) cost plus a certain percentage profit. The amount of profit margin to add to cost takes us back to the discussion on performance ratios in Chapter 6. It was explained there that the return on capital comprises the function of the profit margin on sales and the rate of asset turnover. For example, a 20% return on capital can comprise 2% × 10 = 20% or 10% × 2 = 20% or any number of other combinations. The profit margin to add to cost therefore depends on the return on capital required and the rate of asset turnover anticipated. Suppose a firm aims to achieve a 20% return on capital by earning a 20% profit margin on sales and turning over its assets once only each year. On every product made it therefore needs to earn a 20% profit, but this is not exactly the same as adding 20% to total cost. Without diverging too much into statistics a 20% profit margin on sales, for example, is equal to a 25% addition to total cost as follows:

Total cost	80	
		25% on cost
Profit	20	
		20% on selling price
Selling price	100	

Example

A small printing firm has received an inquiry from a prospective customer for a brochure in quantities of 1,000 copies, 5,000 copies and 10,000 copies. The following information has been compiled by the cost estimator:

	£
Set up cost for this job	560
Material cost per 1,000 brochures	60
Labour cost per 1,000 brochures	50
Overhead recovery based on 280% of the direct labour cost	
Profit margin on sales – 10%	

The quotation for the three possible quantities is best laid out in the form of a simple matrix allowing the relevant information to be fed in as in figure 9.2.

Figure 9.2 Full cost price estimate

Cost item	Number of copies		
	1,000	5,000	10,000
Setting up	560	560	560
Material	60	300	600
Labour	50	250	500
Overhead recovery	140	700	1,400
Total cost (90%)	810	1,810	3,060
Profit – 10% on sales	90	201	340
Selling price (100%)	£900	£2,011	£3,400
Price per brochure	90p	40p	34p

In this example we have applied a global overhead recovery rate based on direct labour cost and quoted selling prices based on total cost. Larger firms would want to channel overheads through departments rather than use one global recovery rate. The charge per brochure falls rapidly with longer print runs because the £560 constant cost of setting up is spread over a greater number of brochures and forms a significant part of total costs.

So far we have applied product costing to a specific job. This system applies to products made to a customer's design as in the engineering and construction industries and in repair services of all kinds, for example, a garage. Firms which produce products in batches also use a variation of the job costing technique when each batch is costed separately.

The other possibility is when production is not of a one-off product or batch but is a continuous process. Examples of process costing are to be found in chemicals and steelmaking. In this case we cannot charge even direct costs to specific units of output so we calculate the average cost of the product. This is achieved by dividing the direct costs for a period of time by the number of units of output in the same period. Overheads are recovered through the departmental analysis and channelling of service department costs through production departments before final absorption by products on a suitable basis. Operating costing is a variation of process costing when the average cost per passenger mile, or per unit of electricity, is calculated.

Inflation

When estimating future overhead costs and possibly some prime costs to establish an overhead recovery rate, full allowance for the anticipated rate of inflation should be made. Similarly, when actually quoting estimates or fixing selling prices, the up-to-date cost of materials and depreciation should be used. To do otherwise will not result in sufficient profit being made to replace the resources consumed at today's prices.

Further reading

Management Accounting, Graham Mott, Pan.
Costing Matters for Managers, E. G. Wood, Business Books.

Self-check questions

1 Total cost = labour + ... + services.
2 Total cost = direct costs + ... costs.
3 Calculate the overhead recovery rate when the estimated overheads for a period are £350,000 and direct labour £120,000.
4 Suggest a suitable basis for apportioning the following overheads:
   (a) Rent and rates. (b) Electricity.
   (c) Employer's pension contributions.
5 What profit mark-up on total cost is required when a firm aims for a 15% return on capital and turns over its capital twice in a year?
6 You have been given the following details for carrying out a job for a new customer:

Direct materials: 7.50 kilos at £10.50 per kilo.
Direct wages:

Department	Hours	Rate per hour
Machine shop	2.0	£5.00
Assembly dept	1.0	£4.00
Packing shop	0.2	£3.00

Annual budget for overheads (recovered on an hourly basis):

Department	Hours	Variable overheads	Fixed overheads
Machine shop	1,000	£20,000	£30,000
Assembly dept	1,500	£15,000	£7,500
Packing shop	800	£10,000	£16,000

Profit: 25% of total cost.

You are required to calculate the charge that should be made for the job based on the details given above. Set out your answer in the form of a statement showing all your calculations.

10 Marginal costing

The previous chapter described the full cost of a product or service as a combination of direct costs and a share of the indirect costs. Marginal costing is a technique which also divides costs into two categories of a somewhat similar nature. In this case costs are identified as being either fixed or variable, relative to the quantity of output. A fixed cost is so called because it does not vary in total when output fluctuates. Rent and rates for a factory, shop or office are good examples of fixed costs. Variable costs are those whose total (not unit cost) varies pro rata with the volume of output. The value of direct materials used on the product or service sold to customers is a typical variable cost.

$$\boxed{\text{TOTAL COST}} \ = \ \boxed{\text{VARIABLE COSTS}} \ + \ \boxed{\text{FIXED COSTS}}$$

The similarity of variable costs to direct costs, and fixed costs to indirect costs, is sometimes a source of confusion. They are not quite the same for a number of reasons. Direct costs usually include the cost of direct labour and materials used on the product itself. Direct material is a variable cost because its cost varies exactly in proportion to the number of products made. This is not always the case with direct labour, particularly in the short term. For example, if a direct labour force is on a guaranteed weekly wage, we cannot say the cost is variable when there is a contractual agreement to pay them a fixed sum irrespective of the level of output achieved. Fixed costs will all be classified as overheads or indirect costs, but some overheads vary pro rata to output. Power, quality inspection and some distribution costs are examples of variable overheads.

It is possible to express fixed and variable costs in the form of a diagram or graph as shown in figure 10.1.

We can often use simple graphs to express the relationship of costs to output and use the graphs as an aid to decision-making. Take the example of two car hire firms. Firm A offers a car at a fixed rate of £10 per day plus 10p for every mile. Firm B charges only £6

Figure 10.1

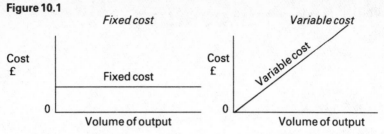

per day but 15p for every mile. The two alternatives can be drawn on one diagram as in figure 10.2. The total cost of using either car comprises the daily fixed charge plus the mileage cost which varies according to miles run:

Figure 10.2 Car hire costs

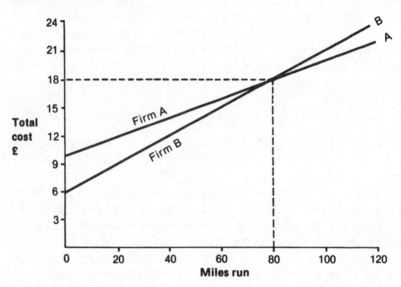

We can conclude from the graph that Firm B is the one to patronise if the daily mileage is expected to be less than eighty miles whilst Firm A should be chosen for mileage in excess of that figure. The total cost is equal where the two lines cross and is called the break-even point. This idea is also used by firms to depict costs, sales revenue and output when the break-even point is that level of output where sales revenue just equals total cost. The firm makes neither a profit nor a loss at this point – hence the use of the term 'break-even'.

Example

A firm makes only one product which sells for £10. The variable cost per unit is £5 and fixed costs total £75,000 per annum. Maximum capacity is 25,000 units per annum but the firm is presently operating at 80% capacity.

Figure 10.3 shows the break-even chart drawn from this information.

Figure 10.3 Break-even chart

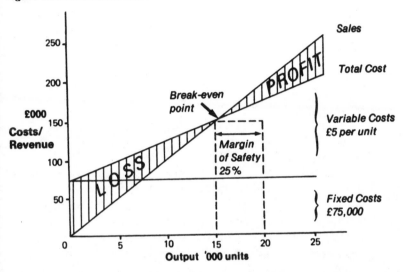

Break-even is reached at 15,000 units when sales just equals total costs of £150,000. Output of less than this amount results in a loss whilst greater output makes a profit. The size of profit or loss at any output can be read off the graph at a glance being the vertical distance between the total cost line and sales line. Also represented on the graph is the margin of safety which represents the proportionate fall in output which can take place before a loss is incurred. In this example, the present level of output of 20,000 units can fall by 25% to 15,000 units before a loss commences. Therefore the margin of safety is 25%.

Although the theoretical distinction between fixed and variable costs is easily understood it is not so easy in practice to separate them. Some costs fall into an in-between category called semi-fixed or semi-variable where there is a fixed amount of cost plus an element which varies with output. One way to separate total costs into fixed and variable types is to graph total costs against the relevant levels of output. If the data covers a number of years the total costs should be updated to today's prices using relevant cost indices. The scattergraph is obtained from plotting total costs against level of output and drawing a line of best fit through the plots. Where the line intersects the vertical line at the origin approximates to the level of fixed costs. Figure 10.4 shows this approach which identifies fixed costs at approximately £200,000.

Figure 10.4 Scattergraph

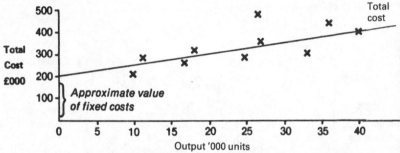

Another reason for the practical difficulty in separating costs into fixed and variable categories is that such analysis varies with time. In the very long run all costs are variable because offices or plants can be closed down and then no further costs will be incurred. In the very short run of a few days, most costs are fixed, apart from direct materials, power and possibly some wages depending on the contracted method of payment.

Although we represent fixed costs as a horizontal line on a break-even chart it is not true to say that fixed costs will remain constant over a wide range of output levels. It could be that more supervisors or managers are required the higher the level of output, or more space or machinery is needed which result in increased

Figure 10.5 Stepped fixed costs

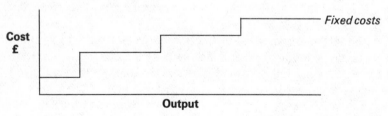

rates or depreciation. Therefore fixed costs may increase in steps as output increases and may correspond more to the picture in figure 10.5 than the horizontal line shown in previous diagrams.

Break-even charts are a useful way of depicting profit or loss at varying levels of output. They can be drawn for a firm as a whole or for one product only. In the latter case the fixed costs are those specifically applicable to the product together with a share of the total to be apportioned over all products.

It is possible to draw a break-even chart in a slightly different manner. If the variable cost is drawn first and then the fixed cost on top, the resultant total cost is the same as if we had represented costs in the original reverse order. The reason for changing the order is to bring out what is known as the 'contribution'. This term is used to describe the difference betwen sales value and variable costs only. It is therefore an intermediate level of profit before fixed costs have been charged.

$$\boxed{\text{SALES}} \; - \; \boxed{\text{VARIABLE COSTS}} \; = \; \boxed{\text{CONTRIBUTION}}$$

We refer to different products making a contribution towards fixed costs and profit by which we mean that they contribute to the common pool from which fixed costs are paid and profit remains.

$$\boxed{\text{CONTRIBUTION}} \; - \; \boxed{\text{FIXED COSTS}} \; = \; \boxed{\text{PROFIT}}$$

Figure 10.6 Contribution break-even chart

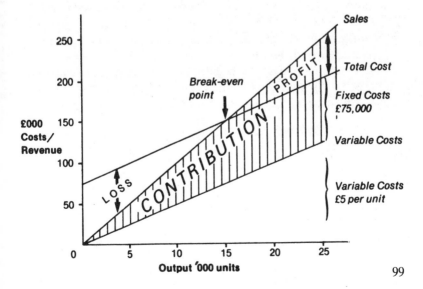

Using the same basic data as for figure 10.3, the break-even chart which identifies contribution as the shaded area is shown in figure 10.6.

The profit and loss areas are still identifiable and break-even point remains the same.

A most important use of the concept of contribution occurs when decisions have to be made concerning product profitability.

Example

Imet Ltd manufactures three products A, B and C of which the first two have been making acceptable profits but C has been losing money for some time. The most recent results for last month are as follows:

	A £000	B £000	C £000	Total £000
Sales	60	120	90	270
less Total costs	42	99	93	234
Profit (loss)	18	21	(3)	36

The directors have considered a number of possible courses of future action but meanwhile have no new products available. Nor can they sell more of products A or B without dropping the selling price. The immediate decision is whether to drop product C and apparently save £3,000 per month.

On investigation by the accountant it is found that the total costs of the products includes £54,000 of fixed costs apportioned £12,000, £24,000 and £18,000 respectively. The fixed costs of £18,000 presently borne by product C will continue irrespective of whether that product is made or discontinued.

A more helpful analysis of the situation is to set out the contribution made by each product to the total fixed costs incurred by the firm and the overall profit achieved. This is shown in figure 10.7.

Figure 10.7 Contribution analysis by products

Product	A £000	B £000	C £000	Total £000
Sales	60	120	90	270
less Variable costs	30	75	75	180
Contribution	30	45	15	90
less Fixed costs				54
Profit				36

The directors of Imet Ltd can now conclude that it is better to continue selling product C for the moment because it is making a contribution of £15,000 towards fixed costs. If product C is discontinued the contributions from the remaining two products will not change, neither will the fixed costs incurred by the firm. Profit will therefore fall by £15,000 to only £21,000 so discontinuing product C immediately is not advisable.

Another use of the concept of contribution is when measuring the profitability of products. If the profitability is measured by expressing the net profit as a percentage of sales, product managers may argue about the unfairness of the apportionment of fixed costs to their own product. Because of the general nature of most fixed costs there is no direct link between them and individual products. One way around this endless debate is to express the contribution as a percentage of sales by calculating what is known as the profit/volume ratio:

$$\text{profit/volume ratio} = \frac{\text{contribution}}{\text{sales}} \%$$

Using the information in figure 10.7 the profit/volume ratios for the three products are calculated as follows:

Product	A	B	C	Total
	£000	£000	£000	£000
Sales	60	120	90	270
Contribution	30	45	15	90
Profit/volume ratio	50%	37½%	16⅔%	33⅓%

Product C is seen to be the least profitable product on this basis.

Product mix

Sometimes firms need to know the particular mix of products which will make the best profit. This situation arises when there are capacity constraints which do not allow the firm to make all the products it can sell. The approach to this problem is to make those products which bring in the highest contribution per unit of scarce resource. Production is allocated to products in their descending order of profitability as measured by '£ *contribution per unit of scarce resource*', be that space, skilled labour, raw materials or anything else.

101

Pricing

The previous chapter explained how firms can fix selling prices based on the total cost of a product plus the profit margin required to earn an acceptable rate of return on capital. An alternative approach is to set the profit/volume ratio required to recover total fixed costs and leave the required profit. For instance, a firm has fixed costs of £200,000 per annum, a profit target of £50,000 and budgeted sales of £600,000. The total contribution required is £250,000 on sales of £600,000 which yields a profit/volume ratio of about 42%. Selling prices can now be set for individual products at a level which leaves a 42% contribution after the variable costs have been deducted. As with full cost pricing there is no guarantee that firms will be able to charge these prices but they do indicate the level of prices needed to achieve a particular return.

Another situation arises in a recession where firms are not able to obtain orders at reasonable prices. Intense competition for scarce orders may result in firms quoting prices which do not fully cover costs. Ship-repairing is sometimes a case in point, being a very cyclical industry. Some repair jobs are very quickly completed so in this situation the only significant variable costs are those for direct materials. Any price in excess of these variable costs will make a contribution towards fixed costs which in this instance will even include direct wages if the labour force are on a guaranteed week.

Obviously no firm can survive very long quoting prices below full cost, or obtaining work whose contribution does not recover fixed costs. In the short term, firms do price work on a less than full cost basis if the alternative is no work at all and even bigger losses.

Changes in volume of output

When calculating product costs on a full cost basis the fixed costs are apportioned over the budgeted volume of output at £X per unit. At higher or lower levels of output the fixed cost per unit is lower or higher respectively, even though fixed costs in total remain the same. It is therefore advisable, when considering changes in output, to leave fixed costs aside and use the contribution approach.

Let us take as an example M Ltd whose directors are considering a 10% reduction in the price of one of their products to increase market share. They wish to maintain profit at the present level by offsetting the volume gain against the price reduction. The present situation is as follows:

Sales of 10,000 units at £20 each	£200,000
Variable costs of £15 per unit	£150,000
Fixed costs	£40,000
Profit	£10,000
	£200,000

The increased volume of sales required at the now lower price of £18 can be calculated from the number of contributions per unit needed to make up the total contribution required:

Contribution per unit = selling price − variable cost
= £18 − £15
= £3
Total contribution required = fixed costs + profit target
= £40,000 + £10,000
= £50,000
Required volume of sales $= \dfrac{\text{total contribution}}{\text{contribution per unit}}$
$= \dfrac{£50,000}{£3}$
= 16,667 units

Therefore to make the same total profit an increase of 67% in volume sales is needed to offset the proposed 10% price reduction.

Further reading

Management Accounting, Graham Mott, Pan.
Management Accounting, N. Thornton, Heinemann.

Self-check questions

1 Draw a break-even chart to decide from which firm you would hire a car. Firm A charges £12.50 per day plus 7p per mile whilst Firm B charges £9 per day plus 10p per mile.
2 Draw the break-even chart shown in figure 10.3 and read off the amount of profit made when output equals 18,000 units.
3 Referring to the information in figure 10.7 would you advise the directors of Imet Ltd to discontinue product C if they could use the same resources to produce 80% more of product A? (Assume same cost and selling price per unit.)
4 Your repair yard has been asked to tender for an immediate repair to a damaged ship, which will provide work for the next few weeks. The yard is short of work, with many men idle,

although being paid a guaranteed wage. You have heard that another firm has already tendered on the basis of direct costs only, without any contribution to overheads or profit. Will you still put in a bid? Give reasons for your answer.

5 A firm sells a product for £25 which has a variable cost of £14. Fixed overheads amount to £800,000 in total and the firm requires a return of 20% on the £1.5m capital employed. How many products need to be sold?

11 Standard costing

Financial information does not always have to be looked at after the events have taken place. It can also be used in a forward planning context. Standard costing is an accounting technique used for the planning and control of costs. The standard cost of a product (or service) is the total cost of labour, materials and overhead apportionment that should be incurred in the production process. When production takes place the actual costs of the batch are compared with the predetermined standard cost for that quantity. Inevitably differences, now called variances, will occur and these are examined for their causes in order to improve future performance.

Firms use standard costing techniques for a variety of reasons. The actual setting-up of the standard cost specification involves determining the most suitable materials and methods of operation from the viewpoints of both firm and consumer. Once set, a standard becomes a yardstick against which performance can be measured. It also engenders cost consciousness in employees who know that costs are being monitored, and hopefully acts as a motivator if the standards are realistically set. Top management can stand back from the day-to-day management which they can delegate and control by investigating only significant variances from standard. Finally, a standard cost is a firm base from which to price products.

Ratios

Before going into the detailed analysis of variances it is useful to look at some measures of company performance associated with the standard costing technique. Central to these measures is the concept of the 'standard hour' which represents the amount of work which can be done in one hour under standard conditions. The standard hour is a useful common denominator with which to aggregate different operations and different products. With this definition we can measure the operating efficiency of a firm by relating the standard hours equivalent of the work produced to the actual hours taken:

$$\text{efficiency ratio} = \frac{\text{standard hours}}{\text{actual hours}} \times \frac{100}{1}\%$$

For example, last week a firm took 500 actual hours to produce goods equivalent to 450 standard hours. Its efficiency ratio for last week is therefore 90%, being adverse compared to the 100% target.

Another ratio is used to measure the level of activity as opposed to the above level of efficiency. The activity ratio relates the actual work produced to the budgeted work for that period, both being expressed in standard hours:

$$\text{activity ratio} = \frac{\text{actual standard hours}}{\text{budgeted standard hours}} \times \frac{100}{1}\%$$

Taking the same example where actual standard hours were 450, let us assume the budgeted standard hours were 475. The activity ratio is therefore 94.7% which again is adverse when 100% is achievable.

A third ratio measures capacity usage by relating actual hours worked in a period to the budgeted standard hours:

$$\text{capacity ratio} = \frac{\text{actual hours}}{\text{budgeted standard hours}} \times \frac{100}{1}\%$$

Using the same figures from the previous illustrations, when 500 actual hours are expressed as a percentage of 475 budgeted standard hours, the capacity ratio is 105.3%. This indicates a favourable variance achieved by somehow working more hours than planned.

Standard cost specification

When applying standard costing to any product the starting point is to specify quantities and grades of the labour and material elements and include an apportionment of budgeted overheads to arrive at total standard cost. The setting of labour and material standards involves determining the best layout, methods of operation and most suitable materials which may lead to economies over previous practice. Management science plays a part here with the application of techniques like method study, work measurement, value analysis and value engineering. An example of a standard cost specification is given in figure 11.1.

Figure 11.1 Standard cost specification

Product: A B Fittings		Batch size: 100 units		
	Quantity	Unit price	Standard cost	
Materials				£
Metal A	40kg	£2.50 per kg	100.00	
Packing cartons	1	25p	25	100.25
Labour				
Operator 1	8 hours	£3.00 per hour	24.00	
Operator 2	12 hours	£2.50 per hour	30.00	
Packer	1 hour	£2.20 per hour	2.20	56.20
Overheads (Standard allowances)				
Variable overheads	21p per unit		21.00	
Fixed overheads	84p per unit		84.00	105.00
Total standard cost				261.45
Standard profit				28.55
Standard selling price				£290.00

Periodically, the actual costs of production are compared with the predetermined standard as laid down in the specification. Variances will be thrown out where the actual cost of some, or all, elements will differ from the standard cost for the quantity actually produced. These variances could be expressed as a $(+)$ or a $(-)$ representing an adverse or favourable result or the symbol letters (A) or (F) used instead. Variances are capable of further analysis, as we shall see, to identify their cause and allow management to take remedial action if necessary. In practice the specification and actual costs are all computerized so that no laborious calculations are required in multi-product firms.

Basically there are only two main types of variance – those relating to unit price and those relating to volume. Referring back to figure 11.1 let us assume a batch of 100 fittings was made recently using 45 kg of metal which had just been purchased for £2.30 per kg. The total material cost variance for metal is the difference between the actual cost and standard cost:

actual cost	–	standard cost	=	material cost variance
45kg×£2.30=£103.50		40kg×£2.50=£100		£3.50 (A)

This £3.50 variance results from two causes and not just one. On the one hand extra costs are incurred through using 5 kg more metal than specified, resulting in a material usage variance of 5 kg×£2.50=£12.50 (A). On the other hand the firm bought the metal more cheaply than it expected and thus saved $20p \times 45\,kg = £9$ (F) which is the material price variance. To summarize:

Total material cost variance		£3.50(A)
Material usage variance	£12.50(A)	
Material price variance	£9.00 (F)	£3.50(A)

Variances for other costs and sales can be similarly divided into two main types and the full list is shown in figure 11.2.

Figure 11.2 Price and volume variances

Price variances	Volume variances
Material price variance	Material usage variance
Labour rate variance	Labour efficiency variance
Variable overhead expenditure variance	—
Fixed overhead expenditure variance	Fixed overhead volume variance
Sales price variance	Sales volume variance

Before looking at a more comprehensive example it is necessary to define each variance carefully and explain it in more general terms:

Material

Material price variance represents the difference in purchase cost caused by a variation in the unit price of the material. It is calculated from the difference between the actual and standard price per unit of material multiplied by the actual quantity purchased.

Formula: $(AP-SP)\,AQ$.

Material usage variance represents the difference in the cost of material used caused by more or less efficient use of that material. It is calculated from the difference between the actual and standard quantity used evaluated at the standard price. In some situations it is possible to analyse this further into mix and yield variances. (Note that any variation from the standard price is contained in the price variance itself.)

Formula: $(AQ-SQ)\,SP$.

Labour

Labour rate variance represents the difference in labour cost caused by any variation from normal rates of pay. It is calculated from the difference between the actual and standard rate per hour multiplied by the actual number of hours paid. Formula: same as material price variances; the rate per hour being the price of labour.

Labour efficiency variance represents the difference in labour

108

cost caused by the degree of efficiency in the use of labour compared with the specified standard. It is calculated from the difference between the actual hours taken and the standard hours allowed evaluated at the standard rate per hour. Formula: same as material usage variance, i.e. $(AQ-SQ)SP$.

Variable overheads

These are overheads whose total cost varies pro rata with the level of production, as opposed to fixed overheads whose total cost does not vary with the production level.

Variable overhead expenditure variance represents the difference between the actual cost and the total amount recovered at the standard rate per unit of output. It is calculated from the difference between actual variable overheads and the quantity of output multiplied by the standard recovery rate per unit. (Note that when variable overheads are recovered on a labour basis, as opposed to a product basis, then a variable overhead efficiency variance can arise.)

Formula: $AC-(AQ\times SR)$.

Fixed overheads

Fixed overhead expenditure variance represents the difference between the actual cost and the estimated or budgeted cost.

Formula: $AC-BC$.

Fixed overhead volume variance represents the under- or over-recovery of fixed overheads caused by the actual volume of production being different to the budgeted volume on which the recovery rate is based. It is calculated from the difference between actual and budgeted volume multiplied by the standard recovery rate per unit.

Formula: $(AQ-BQ)\ SR$.

Sales

Sales price variance represents the profit lost or gained by selling at a non-standard price. It is calculated from the difference between actual and standard selling price multiplied by the actual quantity sold.

Formula: $(AP-SP)\ AQ$.

Sales volume variance represents the profit margins on the difference between actual sales and budgeted sales. It is calculated from the standard profit margin multiplied by the difference between actual sales volume and budgeted sales volume.

Formula: $(AQ-BQ)$ standard profit.

A note of caution should be sounded here. It should not be assumed that all standard costing systems will use the same basis as that shown above. In certain industries using chemicals, the material cost variances are capable of further analysis, as are labour and overhead variances in many other industries. The basis of overhead recovery can also influence the precise method of overhead variance calculation. It is also possible to base a standard costing system on marginal costing principles as briefly outlined at the end of this chapter. Notwithstanding these exceptions, the above analysis of variances provides a very good grounding for most practical systems. A brief example is now taken to demonstrate the calculation of basic material and labour variances.

Example

The standard cost of an article comprises:

Material 'X'	2 kg per article at £5 per kg
Labour	6 hours per article at £3.50 per hour

Last week 400 articles were produced and the actual costs were:

Material 'X'	850 kg at £4.50 per kg
Labour	2,300 hours at £3.50 per hour

From this information we can calculate the material cost variance and the labour cost variance together with their respective price and volume variances:

actual cost	− standard cost	= material cost variance
850×£4.50=£3,825	2×400×£5=£4,000	£175 (F)
material price variance =	(AP−SP) AQ	
	(£4.50−£5) 850=£425 (F) ⎫	
material usage variance =	(AQ−SQ) SP ⎬ £175 (F)	
	(850−800) £5 = £250 (A) ⎭	

The saving of £175 in material costs has two causes. Material 'X' was bought more cheaply than standard, thus saving £425. Possibly because the cheap material was substandard, excessive waste occurred costing £250. Overall the company saved £175, therefore the precise reasons are worth investigating with the purchasing officer and production supervisor respectively.

actual labour cost	− standard labour cost	= labour cost variance
2,300×£3.50=£8,050	6×400×£3.50=£8,400	£350 (F)
labour rate variance	= (AP−SP) AQ	
	(£3.50−£3.50) 2,300=£NIL ⎫	
labour efficiency variance =	(AQ−SQ) SP ⎬ £350 (F)	
	(2,300−2,400) £3.50=£350 (F) ⎭	

There is no rate variance, so the saving in labour cost of £350 is all due to the work force being more efficient than the standard set. Again this is worth investigation with production supervisors to see if lessons can be learned for future occasions.

The ratios and variances mentioned rely on the preparation of budgets detailing planned levels of output, costs and income. This also means that a firm operating a system of standard costing should be able to predict the profit that it will make in a future period from its trading operations. The actual profit it makes will be the same as the budgeted profit if there are no sales or cost variances. Any adverse variances will reduce the actual profit relative to that budgeted, whilst favourable variances will enhance the actual profit. A profit and loss account can be prepared on standard costing lines. This does not show the absolute values of income and expenditure, but the detailed variances which affect the budgeted profit and reconcile it with the actual profit. A more comprehensive example now follows to illustrate this approach.

Example

Carr Chemicals Ltd are a one-product firm. The company uses a standard costing system and prepared the following budget for last week which was expected to result in a profit of £7,000.

Budget for one week

	£	Units	£
Sales at £3 per unit		10,000	30,000
Direct materials			
10,000 kilos at 50p per kilo	5,000		
Direct labour			
5,000 hours at £2.40 per hour	12,000		
Variable overheads			
10,000 units at 25p each unit	2,500		
Fixed overheads			
£3,500 per week (35p each unit)	3,500		
Total cost of sales		10,000	23,000
Budgeted profit at 70p per unit			£7,000

Unfortunately they did not sell as many products as they had planned, as the actual results show, but yet a greater profit was achieved.

111

Actual result for one week

	£	Units	£
Sales at £3.10 per unit		9,000	27,900
Direct materials			
9,500 kilos at 45p per kilo	4,275		
Direct labour			
4,500 hours at £2.45 per hour	11,025		
Variable overhead	2,000		
Fixed overhead	3,250		
Total cost of sales		9,000	20,550
Actual profit			£7,350

We can now draw up a statement reconciling the actual profit with the budgeted profit by detailing the adverse or favourable variances for the week. This shows how the extra profit is achieved.

Profit and loss account for the week

	(F)	(A)	£
Budgeted profit			7,000
Variances:			
Sales price variance (£3.10–£3.00) 9,000	900		
Sales quantity variance (9,000–10,000) 70p		700	
Material price variance (45p–50p) 9,500	475		
Material usage variance (9,500–9,000) 50p		250	
Labour rate variance (£2.45–£2.40) 4,500		225	
Labour efficiency variance (4,500–4,500) £2.40	—	—	
Variable O/H expenditure variance 2,000–(9,000×25p)	250		
Fixed O/H expenditure variance (£3,250–£3,500)	250		
Fixed O/H volume variance (9,000–10,000) 35p		350	
	£1,875	£1,525	350(F)
Actual profit			£7,350

(Note that the standard quantities used in the labour efficiency, material usage and variable overhead expenditure variances are based on the actual production level of 9,000 units.)

Standard marginal costing

It is possible to use a marginal costing approach to standard costing when a standard contribution is determined instead of the standard profit used in a full cost system. The contribution price variance will be identical with the sales price variance representing the profit lost or gained by selling at a non-standard price. Where the two systems differ is that the sales and fixed overhead volume variances are replaced by one contribution volume variance, being the contributions lost or gained on the difference between budgeted volume and the actual volume of activity.

Inflation

The standard cost specification should be based on current prices of the relevant costs. This may lead to periodic revisions of the standard cost and selling price.

Further reading

Management Accounting, Graham Mott, Pan.
Management Accounting, N. Thornton, Heinemann.

Self-check questions

1 What is a standard hour?
2 Define the activity ratio.
3 Name some management techniques which may be used when setting a standard cost specification.
4 Variances are either favourable or ....?
5 Define and give the formula for the labour efficiency variance.
6 The standard cost specification for a product is as follows:

Selling price		£31
less Factory costs		
Direct material – 12 kg at 50p	£6	
Direct labour – 4 hours at £3	£12	
Variable overhead per product	£2	
Fixed overhead per product	£5	£25
Standard profit per product		£6

A firm budgeted to produce and sell 1,100 products last week. Actual production and sales was only 900 and other information is as follows:

Selling price – £32
Direct material – 12,600 kg at 55p
Direct labour – 3,200 hours at £3
Variable overheads £2,100
Fixed overheads £5,700

Produce a statement reconciling the budgeted profit with the actual profit by disclosing all possible variances.

12 Budgetary control

There are many similarities between a system of budgetary control and the standard costing technique discussed in an earlier chapter. They are both concerned with planning and control involving the setting of targets and the later comparison with actual results. Differences, hereafter called variances, arising from such comparisons are identified so that corrective action can be taken as required.

Much detailed preparatory work is common to both budgetary control and standard costing as they are both concerned with detailed costs and revenues. Where the two systems differ is in the unit of application. A standard cost specifies the selling price and cost of a product whilst a budget is prepared for a function or a department. Standard costs are not based on departments because the standard overhead recovery includes costs from all departments, even when the direct costs are incurred in only one department.

Purpose

The main purpose of budgetary control is to plan and control the firm's activities. Corporate and strategic planning are concerned with the long-term broad objectives of the firm. Budgetary control, however, is an expression of financial plans to meet objectives in the coming accounting year. These short-term objectives may be to earn X% return on capital or achieve a certain level of turnover or market share. Although budgets are plans for action in the very near future they must be compatible with what the firm is trying to achieve in the longer term.

Using this system senior management can delegate responsibility to departmental managers and so concentrate solely on deviations from plans without getting overwhelmed by day to day activities that are running smoothly. They are therefore practising the principle of management by exception.

Preparation of budgets

Top management should specify broad objectives to a budget committee comprising representatives of both directors and functional managers. The committee then interprets these objectives into outline plans for each departmental head who in turn submit their detailed proposals. This process may continue a number of times to get the necessary integration and coordination of the individual budget proposals.

When finally accepted by the budget committee, the functional budgets are aggregated into a master budget. This consists of a budgeted profit and loss account for the year, broken down into months, and a projected balance sheet at the year end. If approved by the board this becomes the policy to be pursued for the coming year.

In many firms this procedure, outlined in figure 12.1, is assisted by an accountant or budget officer, who provides information and advice to all concerned. Regrettably, in some firms the complete system of budgetary control is run by accountants for accountants, which consequently loses the motivating aspects of this management tool.

Very small firms may not need a formal committee structure but would do well to set plans down on paper to integrate the functions and see the overall effects in terms of profit and capital requirements.

Figure 12.1 Budget preparation

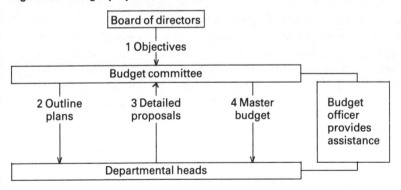

Level of attainment

Thought must be given when setting budgets or standards as to the level of attainment expected. If that level is set too high it will have a demoralizing effect, whilst if set too low it will lead to complacency. The best compromise is to set the level at that attainable by efficient working in the conditions pertaining at the time.

Identification of key factor

The starting point with budgeting is to identify the key factor which limits the firm's growth at this moment in time. In many firms this key factor will be sales volume but it could be a shortage of space, machinery, materials or money. Assuming sales is the key or limiting factor for a firm this places the major responsibility for budgeting on the shoulders of the sales manager or director. The sales team will have to consider the present level of business, anticipate future trading conditions, obtain feedback from sales representatives and market research to come up with a sales budget. This budget is not just one total sales figure for the coming year but must be analysed by customers, by markets, by sales area and by months.

Having specified sales the production budget comes next. The level of production must equate with budgeted sales except when stock levels change. Where stocks are not required, or are kept at a constant level, production and sales volumes will be identical.

Therefore the starting point for budgeting production is the sales budget after taking into account possible changes in stock levels or the use of subcontractors. Production levels must fall within existing capacity as otherwise production would have been identified as the key or limiting factor rather than sales. The production budget specifies the products to be made, when production is to take place, which departments are to be used and the cost of labour, materials and machine time consumed.

Departmental overhead budgets are then prepared based on the level of service needed to allow the sales and production functions to meet their budgets. The production department overheads will be geared to the production levels specified for those departments. Similarly, the selling and distribution costs will be geared to the level of the sales budget whilst the various administrative departments' budgets will be determined by the overall level of activity.

Research and development also has a budget but this is more a long-term investment of funds not closely related to short-term needs and is very similar to the capital budget mentioned below.

Figure 12.2 The budgeting process

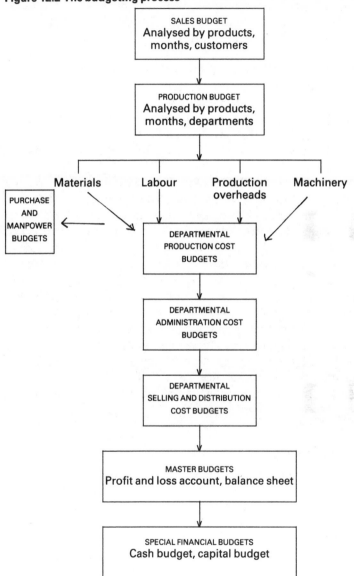

In this way the various functional and departmental budgets are prepared which facilitate the composition of subordinate budgets for material purchases and manpower planning. The functional budgets form the basis for a master budget in the form of a budgeted profit and loss account and projected balance sheet. It is this master budget which goes to the board for approval, and if not satisfactory, the marketing/production mix must be thought through again.

There are two other budgets which it is necessary for the accountant to prepare using his professional skills and applying them to the vast store of financial information prepared in the budgeting process. The cash budget quite literally is a monthly budget of cash inflows and outflows which are expected to arise from the plans expressed in the functional budgets. Details of its preparation and uses are contained in the later chapter on the control of working capital.

A capital budget is a collation of planned capital expenditures on both replacement and new assets. It is partly influenced by the need to replace or buy new assets to facilitate achievement of the coming year's functional budgets. Also included may be capital projects whose expenditure started in a previous year. The total planned expenditure must be within the firm's financial capacity otherwise the available capital must be allocated to the most important categories and most profitable investments. Chapter 14 describes how this profitability is assessed.

Once projects have been approved their progress must be monitored in the capital budget reports by comparing actual costs against those budgeted for the proportion of the work completed. An estimate of 'costs to completion' is also included to give early warning of anticipated cost overruns. A schematic diagram of the budgeting process is shown in figure 12.2.

Budget periods

Budgets are concerned with the planned income and expenditure for the coming year. The accounting year is the natural choice for the budgeting process, although it is broken down into months for regular comparison of actual with budgeted figures. These months may be of the calendar or lunar variety, or some other constant working period to avoid distorted comparisons due to the incidence of works and statutory holidays. Some firms work on a rolling year, adding a new month's budget as each month passes.

Budget reports

The comparison of actual results with budget takes place at two levels. Each departmental manager is fed information about the costs (and income) under his control, comparing actual costs against budget for the month under review and for the cumulative months of the accounting year so far expired. An example of this is given in figure 12.3. Sometimes a distinction is made between controllable costs and costs reallocated to a department although not wholly within the manager's control.

Figure 12.3 Monthly budget report

Cost code	Description	Current month			Cumulative		
		Budget	Actual	Variance	Budget	Actual	Variance
		£	£	£	£	£	£

At a higher level the budgeted profit and loss account is compared with the actual results achieved and reported to the board of directors. When a firm uses a standard costing system the list of variances will link the budgeted profit with the actual profit achieved in the month. Where standard costing is inappropriate to the firm's products, the monthly profit and loss account will compare budgeted costs and revenues with the actual costs and revenues respectively to disclose the variances.

Very small firms will tend to use this approach of comparing detailed profit and loss account items although there is no reason why they should not use standard costing where standardized products are concerned. This is particularly true now that computers are so widely available for such routine tasks.

Significance

There is no point in drawing trivial variances to the attention of departmental managers or directors. Limits may be set as to what counts as a significant variance, being either a percentage of the budgeted figure and/or a certain sum of money. In this way time is not wasted on insignificant events and explanations are only required when a variance is deemed to be important.

Flexible budgeting

The system of budgeting described above is based on fixed budgets which remain unchanged irrespective of the actual level of activity achieved. If the actual level is significantly different from the budgeted level there will be significant 'volume' variances. When standard costing is used, the difference in profit caused by the different level of activity is particularly quantified in the sales volume and fixed overhead volume variances.

In the absence of a standard costing system the solution to the problem of variable levels of activity lies in the use of a flexible budget. This is defined by the Institute of Cost and Management Accountants as a 'budget which is designed to change in accordance with the level of activity attained'. Essentially the flexible budget consists of not one budget, but a series of budgets, each being based on a different level of activity within the expected range. For example, if a firm never expects activity to fall below 70% it can prepare four budgets of income and expenditure at 70%, 80%, 90% and 100% levels of the maximum capacity. Should the actual level turn out to be, say, 83%, then the budget for that level can be derived by interpolating the 80% and 90% budgets. Comparison of actual results can then be made with the budget for the same level of activity. The resulting variances are of a controllable nature as the change in volume has been eliminated.

Flexible budgeting obviously entails the analysis of costs into fixed and variable categories to forecast expenditure at different levels of activity. This is not the same analysis as indirect and direct costs because some indirects vary with the level of activity and some directs, possibly wages, are fixed.

The example in figure 12.4 contrasts the variances arising under a fixed budget system with those obtaining in a flexible budget system. Under the fixed budget system, variances arising from a drop in the level of activity appear as favourable variances. When the budget is 'flexed' to the actual level of activity, actual costs are compared with budgeted costs for the same level of activity. The variances resulting from this comparison are of a controllable nature because by very definition a flexible budget obviates volume or uncontrollable variances.

Figure 12.4 Comparison of fixed and flexible budget systems

1. Illustration of a fixed budget report

	Fixed budget for month	Actual results for month	Variances
Activity	100%	85%	15% (A)
	£	£	£
Direct labour	33,000	31,000	2,000 (F)
Direct materials	27,000	23,700	3,300 (F)
Overheads	36,000	34,100	1,900 (F)
Total	£96,000	£88,800	£7,200 (F)

2. Flexible budget for the same month

Activity	70%	80%	90%	100%
	£	£	£	£
Direct labour	27,000	29,000	31,000	33,000
Direct materials	18,900	21,600	24,300	27,000
Variable overheads	10,500	12,000	13,500	15,000
Fixed overheads	21,000	21,000	21,000	21,000
Total	£77,400	£83,600	£89,800	£96,000

3. Flexible budget report for the same month

	Flexed budget 85%	Actual results 85%	Variances —
	£	£	£
Direct labour	30,000	31,000	1,000 (A)
Direct materials	22,950	23,700	750 (A)
Variable overheads	12,750	12,600	150 (F)
Fixed overheads	21,000	21,500	500 (A)
Total	£86,700	£88,800	£2,100 (A)

Firms may use a mixture of fixed and flexible budgets for different departments. Essentially, the choice is that of fixed budgets fully integrated with a standard costing system to disclose volume variances or flexible budgets where standard costing is inappropriate.

Inflation

Budgets should be prepared on the basis of estimated costs and income over the period, including the size and timing of the anticipated rates of inflation on the various constituents. Should inflation have unforeseen consequences or occur at totally unexpected rates it may be necessary to revise the original budget at a later date. Such action will be a rare event as frequent budget revisions ensure that targets are met!

Further reading

Management Accounting, Graham Mott, Pan.
Management Accounting, N. Thornton, Heinemann.

Self-check questions

1 What is a key or limiting factor in budgeting?
2 What factors would you consider when fixing the sales budget for the coming year?
3 What is a cash budget?
4 What is a flexible budget?
5 What have budgetary control and standard costing systems got in common?
6 A firm has 350 kg of a raw material in stock at the beginning of a budget period. Production will use 10,000 kg of the material during the period and the firm wants the stock level to increase to 750 kg at the end of that time. What quantity must be purchased?

Part 3
Financial management

The way in which a company finances its assets has an effect on the return on owners' capital and the overall cost of capital. Gearing and tax allowances on interest payments can enhance the return on shareholders' funds but carry risks if taken too far.

Capital is invested in either fixed assets or in working capital. This part of the book examines the techniques of investment appraisal which assist in the decision of whether, when and where to deploy scarce resources. The management of stocks, debtors and cash which make up working capital is also explored.

Both the raising of capital and its use affect the share price of a private sector company through the impact on reported profit. Different ways of valuing company shares are discussed before examining their role in merger and takeover situations.

Finally, the taxation of business profits is outlined under the systems of corporation tax for limited companies and income tax for self-employed persons. The UK is a predominant trader with other countries and the peculiarities of overseas, as opposed to home, trade are reviewed.

13 The cost of capital

Capital is not free. The owners of firms and financial institutions require a return on their investment in the company. In turn the company must earn a return on assets at least equal to this cost of capital. To do otherwise will not satisfy the providers of that capital and will make the raising of future capital more difficult, if not impossible.

Firms need to set a minimum required rate of return against which the profitability of proposed new investments is measured. This required rate must at least be equal to the cost of the different types of capital used in the business.

There are two main sources of new capital for new investments. Firms can either borrow the money, usually from a financial institution, or they can obtain it from the owners. In this latter case new equity capital can be obtained in one of two ways. Companies occasionally sell new shares to existing shareholders on a 'rights' issue. This may be unpopular as it tends to depress the existing share price on the Stock Exchange. The other way companies obtain new capital from the owners is by not paying out all the profits earned as dividends. By this means companies are assured of the extra capital they need and they save the expense of issuing new shares.

Most firms use a mix of borrowed and owners' capital and the relationship between the two is known as 'capital gearing'. A company is said to be highly geared when it has a large amount of borrowed capital relative to owners' capital. It is lowly geared when the proportion of borrowed capital is small. Strictly speaking gearing is the use of any prior charge capital including preference

Figure 13.1 Example of high and low capital gearing

	(a) Low gearing	(b) High gearing
Owners' capital (share capital+retained profits)	90%	50%
Borrowed capital	10%	50%
Total capital	100%	100%

shares. The relationship between these two sources of capital is also expressed by calculating each source as a proportion of the total capital. The two situations in figure 13.1 illustrate different levels of gearing.

There is no one particular level of capital gearing that is regarded as satisfactory for all companies. Each firm is examined on its past record, future prospects and the security of the interest and capital repayments. In most industries the 50% borrowed capital indicated in figure 13.1(b) would be regarded as very high, although much higher rates are not uncommon in the rather special case of property development.

It is possible to find examples of companies with no borrowed capital, resulting from a policy decision by management to finance growth internally from retained profits. Such companies eliminate the risks of defaulting on the loan or interest repayments, or having to reduce dividends to make interest payments when profits fall. On the other hand they miss the opportunity of increasing the return to ordinary shareholders by investing borrowed capital to earn more than the cost of the interest, as figure 13.2 shows.

Figure 13.2 Illustration of the effects of capital gearing

	Nil gearing £000	High gearing £000
Capital structures		
Ordinary shares of £1	2,900	1,400
Retained profits	1,000	1,000
10% loan stock	—	1,500
	3,900	3,900
Profit of £600,000		
Profit	600	600
Interest	—	150
	600	450
Corporation tax at 35%	210	157
Earned for ordinary shareholders	390	293
Return on ordinary shareholders' funds	10%	12%
Profit of £1,200,000:		
Profit	1,200	1,200
Interest	—	150
	1,200	1,050
Corporation tax at 35%	420	367
Earned for ordinary shareholders	780	683
Return on ordinary shareholders' funds	20%	28%

When a company has no gearing the change in the profit results in the same proportionate change in the return on shareholders' funds. In the *nil* gearing example, doubled profits also double the return to the owners from 10% to 20%. The doubling of the same profit in the high gearing example more than doubles the return on ordinary shareholders' funds from 12% to 28%.

Most firms decide that a judicious amount of borrowed capital is beneficial and try to adhere to a target level of gearing over the years. It may be that in any one year the target is exceeded because conditions in the capital markets do not allow a particular kind of funding to take place. This can be redressed as soon as market conditions allow.

New projects must be financed by new capital, as opposed to existing capital which has already been spent on existing projects. We therefore need to look at the cost and the mix of new capital to calculate the minimum required rate of return on new investments. Also we must bear in mind the effects of taxation and inflation on each type of capital as they differ in certain respects. We will first examine the cost of borrowed capital, then the cost of equity, and weight the different proportions to get an overall cost.

The cost of borrowed capital

The rate of interest which has to be paid on new loans to get them taken up by investors at par can be regarded as the cost of borrowed capital. Such rates of interest vary over time in sympathy with interest rates obtainable on alternative investments. They also vary slightly according to the size of the loan and the degree of risk attached to the particular firm.

An alternative approach can be used to find the current cost of borrowing for a firm which has existing quoted loans or debentures. If the fixed rate of interest on such loans is less than the current going rate, these securities will have a market price of less than the par value of the stock. This means investors will obtain an annual return from the interest payments and a capital gain on the eventual repayment of the stock at par.

Suppose X Ltd has a 10% loan stock standing at £83 per £100 nominal value, repayable at par in five years' time. An investor today is therefore willing to pay £83 for the right to receive £10 yearly interest for the next five years and his £100 back at the end of that time. We can approach this in the way we calculate the discounted cash flow (DCF) yield on industrial investments as explained in the next chapter. Figure 13.3 shows this to be 15%.

Figure 13.3 Calculation of the DCF yield on the investment of £83 in £100 of 10% loan stock repayable in five years' time

Year	Cash flow £	PV factors at 15%	PV £
0	− 83	1.000	−83.00
1	+ 10	.870	+ 8.70
2	+ 10	.756	+ 7.56
3	+ 10	.658	+ 6.58
4	+ 10	.572	+ 5.72
5	+110	.497	+54.67
			+£0.23

The DCF yield of 15% obtained by an investor buying the company's existing loan stock can be regarded as the current cost of interest on new loans issued at par. It represents the money or nominal cost of new loans, which is used to calculate the target rate of return in nominal terms. The real cost of loan capital will be significantly less as investors are not compensated for the fall in the value of their capital. This is the reason for the 'gearing adjustment' in the inflation-adjusted profit and loss account. In the 1970s this real cost of loan capital was negative after allowing for both inflation and the tax relief next mentioned.

Interest on loans, debentures and overdrafts is deductible from profits before calculating the corporation tax charge, whereas dividends are not. In effect tax relief is granted on interest payments which, with corporation tax at 35%, reduces the rate of interest by about one-third. Figure 13.4 illustrates this point.

Figure 13.4 Illustration of tax relief on interest payments

	Company A (no gearing)		Company B (50% gearing)
Shareholders' funds	£10m		£5m
10% loan	—		£5m
Total capital employed	£10m		£10m
Profit before tax and interest	£2,000,000		£2,000,000
Interest on loan	—		£ 500,000
Profit after interest	£2,000,000		£1,500,000
Corporation tax at (say) 35%	£ 700,000		£ 525,000
Tax saved		£175,000	

127

It can be seen that two companies with identical total capitals and annual profits do not pay the same tax charge. Company B which financed half of its capital requirement from a 10% loan saves £175,000 of the £500,000 interest cost through tax relief. The effective rate of interest on the loan is therefore only 6.5% ($\frac{£0.325\text{m}}{£5.000\text{m}} \times \frac{100}{1}\%$). It is not surprising that firms find gearing attractive when they compare the after-tax cost of loans with the cost of equity capital!

The cost of equity capital

The equity of a company is its risk capital, embracing ordinary share capital and retained profits which can be regarded as having the same cost. Companies retain profits to short-circuit paying out all profits with one hand whilst asking shareholders to buy new shares with the other. There is clearly a saving in administrative costs and professional fees by retaining profits, so this alternative will be slightly cheaper in practice.

Put simply, the cost of equity is the return shareholders expect the company to earn on their money. It is their estimation, often not scientifically calculated, of the rate of return which will be obtained both from future dividends and an increased share value. Unfortunately, simple concepts are not always so easy to apply in practice and the cost of capital is a favourite battlefield for academics with no one agreed practical solution.

It is possible to calculate the cost of equity as the DCF yield achieved from the estimated future dividends and the increased share value at a future point of time. This corresponds to the approach used to calculate the cost of borrowed capital in figure 13.3. An alternative approach is to take the current dividend yield for a company and add the expected annual growth. For example, Graham Ltd currently pay a net dividend of 10p on each ordinary share which is quoted at £2 on the Stock Exchange. Growth of profits and dividends has averaged 15% over the last few years. The cost of equity for Graham Ltd can be calculated as:

$$\text{cost of equity capital} = \frac{\text{current net dividend}}{\text{current market price}}\% + \text{growth rate}\%$$

$$= \left(\frac{10\text{p}}{£2} \times \frac{100}{1}\% \right) + 15\%$$

$$= \quad 20\%$$

With this method, dividends are assumed to grow in the future at the constant rate achieved by averaging the last few years' performance. This growth is best calculated from profits after tax, rather than dividends, as changes in company dividend policy or government controls over dividend payments can distort short-term trends. No residual share price is included as it is assumed that dividend payments continue to perpetuity. The 20% cost of equity capital above is a nominal rate rather than a real rate of return to investors. It is an after-tax return as dividends are paid from taxed profits, unlike interest payments which are allowed against tax.

Another way to calculate the cost of equity is to calculate the 'earnings yield' which was a popular method in the past. The term 'earnings yield' is akin to the dividend yield but in this case it refers to profit irrespective of whether it is paid out as dividend or retained by the company.

For example, Graham Ltd made a profit of £20m last year which is expected to be maintained. There are 50m ordinary shares in issue and they currently sell at £2 each on the Stock Exchange. The earnings yield and therefore the cost of equity at 20% can be calculated from:

$$\text{earnings per share} = \frac{\text{profit for year}}{\text{no. of ordinary shares}} = \frac{£20m}{50m} = 40p$$

$$\text{earnings yield} = \frac{\text{earnings per share } \%}{\text{market price}} = \frac{40p}{£2} = 20\%$$

A more recent approach to the cost of equity tries to take the risk element into account. Known as the 'capital asset pricing model', a particular company's share performance is measured against the whole market performance for a period of years. In both cases the risk-free return earned on short-dated government securities is excluded so that the risk premium or discount against the market generally can be ascertained. The nominal cost of equity capital for any one company therefore comprises the after-tax risk-free return plus the market risk premium plus the company risk premium (or discount) against the market.

It is unlikely that all the above techniques will coincide but it is also unlikely that there will be very wide divergence. We must always remember that a precise calculation will only really matter for marginal projects rather than the vast majority of schemes which are either more than marginally profitable, or totally unviable. Having decided on the cost of equity we can reassure ourselves by conducting a few simple tests. The cost of equity should be more than the pre-tax cost of borrowed capital because of the greater element of risk. Taken over only one year this does not appear to be the case as evidenced by the 'reverse yield gap' which measures the excess of the current fixed interest rate over the current dividend yield on shares. As dividends can increase in future years whereas interest remains fixed, this results in the cost of equity exceeding the cost of borrowed capital when taken to perpetuity.

Another comparison we can make is to look at the shareholder's opportunity cost if he made alternative investments. If the cost of equity appears lower than the return achievable on other financial securities of equal or lesser risk, we should go back to the drawing board. Either the calculation of the cost of equity is incorrect or we cannot justify investing more equity capital to achieve a lower return than shareholders expect.

New projects are financed by a mix of borrowed capital and equity capital. Having determined their separate costs we now need to combine them together to calculate the weighted average cost of capital at the desired level of capital gearing.

Weighted average cost of capital

Let us assume Canny Ltd attempt to keep their gearing ratio of borrowed capital to shareholders' funds in the proportion of 15:85. The nominal cost of new capital from these sources has been assessed, say, at 10% and 20% respectively. We now need to take account of the tax relief on interest, the cost of each type of new capital, and the mix of types to calculate the overall cost as follows:

Figure 13.5 Calculation of the nominal weighted average cost of capital

Type of capital	Proportion	After-tax cost	Weighted cost
10% loan capital	0.15	× 6.5%	= 1.0%
Shareholders' funds	0.85	× 20.0%	= 17.0%
	1.00		18.0%

The resulting weighted average cost of 18% is the minimum rate which Canny Ltd will accept on proposed investments. Any investment which is not expected to achieve an 18% return is not a viable proposition for this firm. When firms weight the cost of capital for risk by adding a risk premium, this may result in a substantially higher target being set for some projects.

New investments are financed from a pool of funds rather than from one particular source, except in the case of particularly large projects. This pool is composed primarily of borrowed and owners' capital together with depreciation and other retained profits. We can think of depreciation as retained profit for the specific purpose of helping to replace any assets that have worn out during the year. Such asset replacements allow those projects to continue to earn a return provided this is still satisfactory. When we appraise replacements we can use the current cost of capital to choose between alternative replacements and to decide when the replacement should take place.

The next chapter discusses how firms appraise new investments.

Further reading

Investment Appraisal, Graham Mott, Pan.
Management of Company Finance, J. M. Samuels and F. M. Wilkes, Van Nostrand Reinhold.

Self-check questions

1 What is meant by a high level of 'gearing'?
2 Using the illustration in figure 13.2, calculate the return on ordinary shareholders' funds in the high gearing case when the profit is £1,000,000 and the tax rate is 50%.
3 What is the current cost of interest on a new loan if a firm has an existing 8% loan repayable in three years' time and quoted at £75 per £100 nominal value?
4 What is the after-tax cost of interest for a company paying 35% rate of corporation tax if it pays 12% interest on a bank loan?
5 Canny Ltd ordinary shares sell at £1.50 at the present time and the growth of profits and dividends has averaged 10% per annum in recent years. What is its cost of equity capital if the latest dividend was 8p net?
6 What is the 'reverse yield gap'?
7 Calculate the nominal weighted average cost of capital in figure 13.5 when the proportion of loan capital to shareholders' funds is 0.4:0.6.

14 Capital investment appraisal

Investment appraisal is concerned with decisions about whether, when and how to spend money on capital projects. Such decisions are important ones for the companies involved because often large sums of money are committed in an irreversible decision, with no certain knowledge of the size of future benefits.

Suppose a printing firm is considering buying a binding machine for £10,000 which will reduce labour costs on this activity by £3,000 every year for each of the five years the machine is expected to last. What the management of this firm have to consider – and this is no easy task – is whether a return of £3,000 every year for five years justifies the initial investment of £10,000.

The essence of all investment appraisals is to measure the worth-whileness of proposals to spend money, by comparing the benefits with the costs. If this measurement is done badly, it can hamper a firm's growth and employment prospects for years to come, and may lead to an inability to attract new investors. Financial institutions and individuals provide firms with capital in the expectation of a reasonable rate of return. If a firm invests that money in projects which do not yield a reasonable return then investors will be wary of that company in the future. The minimum return required on new investments will be the cost of capital as calculated in the previous chapter.

We measure the worthwhileness of investment proposals by building simple financial models of the expected events. Using the binding machine example above we can set out the expected events

Figure 14.1 Financial model of the binding machine project

	£
Year 0	−10,000
Year 1	+ 3,000
Year 2	+ 3,000
Year 3	+ 3,000
Year 4	+ 3,000
Year 5	+ 3,000
Total profit	+£5,000

as cash inflows or outflows for each year of the machine's life, as in figure 14.1. These cash flows start at Year 0 which is the beginning of the first year when the project is initiated.

Types of investment situation

There are a number of basic situations where an appraisal takes place:

- Expansion – assessing the worthwhileness of expanding existing product lines requiring additional investment in buildings, plant, stocks, debtors, etc.
- New product/diversification – assessing the viability of the more risky investment in totally new products.
- Cost saving – assessing the profitability of a cost-saving scheme: for example, when an investment in a new machine automates an existing manual process.
- Replacement – deciding whether and when to replace an old machine with a new one to save operating costs or reduce wastage.
- Alternative choice – deciding between alternative investments to achieve the same ends; for example, choosing between two or more machines with different financial characteristics.
- Financing – comparing the cost of purchasing an asset outright with the alternative cost of leasing.

All the above investment situations have the same common approach. In each case we must decide whether the benefits we get from the initial investment are sufficient to justify the original capital outlay.

There may be some investment situations where no benefits are quantifiable in money terms. For example, the government may require firms to invest in fire detection and alarm systems in all their premises. In this case firms have no choice, and although there will be benefits in employee welfare these are not readily quantifiable in cash terms. Even in this kind of situation an appraisal technique could be used to help us make the choice between competing systems which have different financial characteristics. In the case of the fire detection and alarm system, one supplier's equipment may have a high capital cost but a low maintenance cost over a long life. An alternative supplier's equipment may have a low capital cost but high maintenance costs over a short life. We need to formalize this information to make a rational judgement.

All appraisal methods require an estimate of the yearly cash flows attributable solely to the project under review. Typically there will be an initial cash outflow on a project, being the cash spent on the physical assets like buildings, plant, vehicles, machinery and the like. If any of these items need replacing before the project ends, then a cash outflow will also occur in that later year. Other cash outflows may occur through the firm building up stocks or giving credit to its customers. These working capital items will be cash outflows at the beginning of the project or at some subsequent date if increased in amount. At the end of a project the working capital is released and becomes a cash inflow at that time.

Cash inflows occur, for example, from sales revenue less their wage and material costs. No deduction from such income is made for depreciation as the total asset cost is shown as a cash outflow. Where cost-saving projects are concerned, the cash inflow each year is the value of these cost savings, again without charging any depreciation. The cost of the investment will be shown in full as a cash outflow at the time of acquisition. It is worth emphasizing at this point that profits which accrue from cost-saving investments are just as valuable as profits from investments extending the firm's output.

At this stage all cash flows are expressed in £s of Year 0 purchasing power and inflation is ignored. A brief description of how to cope with inflation follows later but first is needed a review of the four main methods used to appraise investment projects.

Investment appraisal methods

Two of the methods are relatively crude measures of the worth-whileness of an investment and this sums up their weakness. The remaining methods are much more precise as they are both based on yearly interest calculations. They are easy techniques to understand and with the help of modern computers and calculators are not difficult to implement. In recent years more and more firms have been adopting these interest-based methods of appraisal although some firms may retain a payback requirement in addition. It should be appreciated that only these latter methods can adequately incorporate taxation, inflation and uncertain future events.

Payback method

Simplicity is the keynote of this investment appraisal method. Payback measures the number of years it is expected to take to recover the cost of the original investment.

As an illustration let us assume that the board of directors of the printing firm mentioned in figure 14.1 set a maximum period of three years within which any investment must be paid back. Payback in this example will take just over three years to complete and the investment will be rejected. One disadvantage of this method is that cash received after payback is completed is totally ignored. Another disadvantage is that no attempt is made to relate the total cash earned on the investment to the amount invested. The payback method does not attempt to measure this total profitability over the whole life of the investment and other methods have to be introduced to do this. However, payback is still used and can yield useful information as an indicator of risk, but is best used in conjunction with other methods.

Rate of return method

The rate of return used to be the main method of investment appraisal as it purports to measure exactly what is required, namely, the annual profit as a percentage of the capital invested.

An average profit is calculated by taking the total profits earned on the investment over the whole of its life and dividing by the expected life of the project in years. Profit in this context is after charging the total cost of the investment or wholly depreciating it in accountants' terminology. This total profit is more easily understood as the total cash inflows less the total cash outflows. The average investment is normally regarded as half the original investment on the grounds that it will be wholly depreciated by the end of its useful life. Referring again to figure 14.1, the average profit is £1,000 and the average investment £5,000 giving a rate of return of 20% per annum for five years.

A disadvantage of this method is that the calculation can give misleading results. Provided total profits were £5,000 over the five years, the return will be 20% irrespective of whether the cash flows increased, decreased or stayed constant as in the example. The method does not take timing into account. Nor will it help rank projects whose lives vary, as the rates of return cannot be directly compared in this case.

At a later stage it will also become apparent that the average investment is a statistical illusion. One reason is that the cost of the investment is often quickly reduced by the early receipt of tax allowances and, possibly, regional development grants. If these benefits are averaged out over the life of the investment they will not be shown at their true worth to the firm.

True rate of return

The profitability of an investment should be measured by the size of the profit earned on the capital invested. This is what the rate of return method attempts to do without perfect success. An ideal method will not rely on averages but will relate these two factors of profit and capital employed to each other in every individual year of the investment's life.

A useful analogy can be made with a building society mortgage. In this situation the borrower pays to the society a sum of money each year. Part of this sum is taken as interest to service the capital outstanding, leaving the remainder as a capital repayment to reduce the capital balance. The profitability of the investment from the society's viewpoint can be measured by the rate of the interest payment, assuming that the yearly capital repayments have paid off all the mortgage.

Figure 14.2 sets out the yearly cash flows of a typical building society mortgage of £20,000 repayable over ten years with interest at 12% per annum on the reducing balance. The small surplus remaining at the end of ten years is negligible given the size of the annual cash flows.

Figure 14.2 £20,000 mortgage at 12% p.a. repayable over ten years

	Annual cash flow £	Interest payment at 12% p.a. £	Capital repayment £	Capital balance outstanding £
Year 0	−20,000			20,000
1	+ 3,540	2,400	1,140	18,860
2	+ 3,540	2,263	1,277	17,583
3	+ 3,540	2,110	1,430	16,153
4	+ 3,540	1,938	1,602	14,551
5	+ 3,540	1,746	1,794	12,757
6	+ 3,540	1,531	2,009	10,748
7	+ 3,540	1,290	2,250	8,498
8	+ 3,540	1,020	2,520	5,978
9	+ 3,540	717	2,823	3,155
10	+ 3,540	379	3,161	6 (surplus)

This building society is getting a true return of 12% p.a. on the reducing capital balance of the mortgage.

Present value

The calculations involved in proving the building society's return on investment to be 12% are somewhat laborious. A simpler method is used in practice based on the principles of compound interest. Suppose £1 was invested one year ago at interest of 10% per annum. After one year the sum has grown to £1.10. If the £1 was invested two years ago it would have grown to £1.21 with the first year's interest reinvested. Compound interest measures the *future value* of money invested sometime in the past. It is equally possible to look at money in the reverse direction, namely, the *present value* of money receivable at a future point in time. The present value of a future sum of money is the equivalent sum now that would leave the recipient indifferent between the two amounts. The present value or equivalent sum to £1 receivable in one year's time is that amount which if invested for one year would accumulate to £1 in one year's time. Using a 10% rate of interest, £1 receivable in one year's time has an equivalent value now of £0.909 because £0.909 invested for one year at 10% will accumulate to £1.

The following is an extract from the present value table shown in Appendix 4 compared with the compound interest factors at the same rate of interest:

Figure 14.3

	Present value of £1 receivable in a future year with interest at 10%	Future value of £1 with compound interest at 10%
Year 0 (now)	1.000	1.000
1	.909	1.100
2	.826	1.210
3	.751	1.331
4	.683	1.464

The relationship between the factors is that one is the reciprocal of the other for the same year. For example, for Year $4 \frac{1}{.683} = 1.464$.

Returning to the building society mortgage illustrated in figure 14.2, this was shown to have a true rate of profitability of 12%. This can now be proved using the simpler present value approach as in figure 14.4. To do this the cash flows are tabulated yearly and brought back (discounted) to their present value by the use of present value

137

factors. In effect, interest is deducted for the waiting time involved. The remaining cash is therefore available to repay the original investment. The profitability of the investment is measured by the maximum rate of interest which can be deducted, whilst leaving just enough cash to repay the investment. This rate of interest is the same 12% as found in figure 14.2. The surplus of £3 is negligible given the size of the annual cash flows.

Figure 14.4 Calculation of the rate of profitability of a £20,000 mortgage repayable over ten years with interest of 12% p.a. using present value factors

	Annual cash flow £	Present value factors at 12%	Present value £	
Year 0	−20,000	1.000		−20,000
1	+ 3,540	.893	+3,161	
2	+ 3,540	.797	+2,821	
3	+ 3,540	.712	+2,520	
4	+ 3,540	.636	+2,251	
5	+ 3,540	.567	+2,007	
6	+ 3,540	.507	+1,795	
7	+ 3,540	.452	+1,600	
8	+ 3,540	.404	+1,430	
9	+ 3,540	.361	+1,278	
10	+ 3,540	.322	+1,140	+20,003
				+ £3

The rate of profitability on this investment is 12%.

The effect of using present value (PV) factors on the future cash flows is to take compound interest off for the waiting time involved. If a higher rate of interest than 12% was applied in figure 14.4 then not all the capital would be repaid over the ten-year life. If a lower rate of interest than 12% was used, the capital repayments would be larger each year as the present values would be larger. This would result in the mortgage being repaid in less than the ten years stipulated.

Both the methods of calculation explained above in figures 14.2 and 14.4 arrive at the same conclusion, although at first sight they may not appear related. That they are related can be seen by comparing the capital repayments in figure 14.2 with the inverted present values in figures 14.4 which are almost identical apart from rounding off differences. This will always be the case in examples with constant annual cash flows. The present value approach will also give correct results with any fluctuating pattern of annual cash flows.

Net present value method

We can use this present value approach to assess the profitability of investment projects. For example, the directors of E Ltd are considering investing £150,000 on a press to make and sell an industrial fastener. Profits before charging depreciation (i.e. cash inflows) are expected to be £60,000 for each of the first four years tapering off to £40,000 in Year 5 and only £20,000 in Year 6 when the press will be scrapped. E Ltd normally require a minimum rate of return of 20%.

The cash flows can be set out and multiplied by the present value factors at 20% to demonstrate whether this project meets the 20% required rate as in figure 14.5.

Figure 14.5 Calculation of the net present value at 20%

	Annual cash flow	PV factors at 20%		PV
	£			£
Year 0	−150,000	1.000		−150,000
1	+ 60,000	.833	+49,980	
2	+ 60,000	.694	+41,640	
3	+ 60,000	.579	+34,740	
4	+ 60,000	.482	+28,920	
5	+ 40,000	.402	+16,080	
6	+ 20,000	.335	+ 6,700	+178,060
			NPV	+£28,060

The net present value (NPV) surplus of £28,060 means that the rate of return is more than the 20% rate of interest used. This is because the annual cash flows are big enough to allow more interest to be deducted and still repay the original investment.

The word 'net' in net present value means the sum of the negative and positive present values and this method of investment appraisal is widely known as the net present value method or NPV method for short.

Discounted cash flow yield method

The NPV method answers the question of a projects viability when tested against the required rate of return of that particular company. This required rate is alternatively referred to as the criterion rate, or cut-off rate, being 20% in the above example for E Ltd.

Sometimes managers want to know not just whether a project is viable, but what rate of return they can expect on a project. To answer this question the NPV method is taken a stage further. The annual cash flows in E Ltd are discounted again at a higher trial rate of interest. Such trial is an educated guess but a higher rather than a lower rate is chosen because of the NPV surplus which previously occurred.

Assuming a trial rate of 30% was chosen then the annual cash flows can be discounted by the present value factors at 30% as in figure 14.6.

Figure 14.6 Calculation of the net present value at 30%

	Annual cash flow	PV factors at 30%	PV	
	£			£
Year 0	−150,000	1.000		−150,000
1	+ 60,000	.769	+46,140	
2	+ 60,000	.592	+35,520	
3	+ 60,000	.455	+27,300	
4	+ 60,000	.350	+21,000	
5	+ 40,000	.269	+10,760	
6	+ 20,000	.207	+ 4,140	+144,860
			NPV	− £5,140

As there is a deficit net present value of £5,140 the rate of return is less than 30%. This is because too much interest has been deducted to allow all the capital to be repaid. If instead of going to an estimated trial rate of 30% the annual cash flows had been repeatedly discounted at 1% intervals from the 20% required rate then a zero net present value would have been found at about 28%. This is the true rate of return on the project and is known as the discounted cash flow yield. In other words the DCF yield is the solution rate of interest which when used to discount annual cash flows on a project gives an NPV of zero.

Interpolation

It would be a tedious task to adopt the above method of successive discounting at 1% intervals but fortunately this is not required. The NPV calculation at 20% and 30% yielded a surplus of £28,060 and a deficit of £5,140 respectively. This provides sufficient information to estimate the DCF yield reasonably accurately by interpolation, which can then be proved by calculation. The interpolation shows:

$$20\% + \left(\frac{28,060}{28,060+5,140} \times (30\% - 20\%) \right) = 28.5\%.$$

Another interpolation method takes the form of a simple graph with the rate of interest on the vertical axis and the net present value on the horizontal axis. The NPVs from the trial at the company's required rate and the further 'guesstimate' are then plotted against their respective interest rates and the two plots joined by a straight line. The approximate DCF yield is where the straight line intersects the vertical axis at a zero NPV. If the two plots are far removed from the actual rate of return the interpolation may not be quite accurate and it should be proved by a final calculation.

It is possible to calculate the DCF yield to one or more decimal places. Although one decimal place may be justifiable there is usually no case for further precision. This is because the basic data on which the calculations are performed are only estimates of future events. To calculate the DCF yield to, say, three decimal places gives an impression of precision which is illusory.

Other short cuts

The interpolation techniques described earlier are obvious short cuts in the search for the solution rate of interest. Some managers may have access to calculators or computers which can rapidly answer the question of a project's rate of profitability. Another short cut is applicable where there is a constant annual cash flow in every year of the project's life. This method is based on the principle that if a constant cash flow is multiplied by individual PV factors the total present value will be the same as if the constant annual cash flow had been multiplied by the sum of the individual PV factors.

If the sum of the individual PV factors had to be arrived at by literally adding up the individual factors this might be thought to be a long short cut! Fortunately a table exists with all the adding up done for the reader and the total of any number of individual year factors can be read off at a glance. Such a table is shown in full in Appendix 5 as the present value of £1 receivable annually or, put more simply, a cumulative PV table.

Such cumulative PV tables can be used as short cuts to both the

NPV and DCF yield. Because the cumulative table applies only to constant annual cash flows this technique is usually used for rule-of-thumb calculations on a project's profitability. Very often managers or industrial engineers want a quick guide as to whether it is profitable to pursue a certain course of action. This can easily be done using a cumulative PV table when the cash flows are relatively constant. A more comprehensive evaluation incorporating taxation, grants, working capital changes, etc, can be done later.

Take for example a proposal to introduce a fork-lift truck to handle palletized stock in a warehouse at a cost of £50,000. This can be expected to yield an annual saving in labour costs less truck running costs of £18,500. The equipment is expected to last six years and the company regards a 25% return before tax as a minimum requirement.

Figure 14.7 Calculation of the NPV on a fork-lift truck project

	Annual cash flow £	Cumulative PV factors at 25%		PV £
Year 0	−50,000	1.000		−50,000
1–6	+18,500	2.951		+54,594
			NPV	+£4,594

The project satisfies the required rate of 25%.

The above method quickly solves the NPV but can be used to even greater effect in finding the DCF yield. Here we require the cumulative PV factor to be first calculated and then looked up on the line of the relevant year of the cumulative PV table, in this case Year 6. Continuing with the fork-lift truck example the cumulative PV factor which gives an NPV of zero must be equal to £50,000 ÷ £18,500. This is the cost of the investment divided by the constant annual return which equals 2.703. On the Year 6 line of the cumulative PV table 2.703 almost exactly equates with the cumulative factor of 2.700 at 29% which is therefore the size of the DCF yield.

Comparison of appraisal methods

Four methods of investment appraisal have been discussed so far and useful conclusions can be drawn by comparing these four methods on the same projects. Figure 14.8 sets out three projects with different lives and different patterns of cash flow and appraises

Figure 14.8 Appraisal methods compared

	Project A		Project B		Project C	
	£		£		£	
Year 0		−200,000		−200,000		−200,000
1	+20,000		+80,000		+60,000	
2	+40,000		+60,000		+60,000	
3	+60,000		+60,000		+60,000	
4	+60,000		+40,000	+240,000	+60,000	
5	+60,000		—		+40,000	
6	+68,000	+308,000	—		+20,000	+300,000
Total profit		+108,000		+ 40,000		+100,000
Payback period (ranking BCA)		4⅓ years		3 years		3⅓ years
Rate of return (ranking ACB)		18%		10%		16.7%
NPV@12% (ranking CAB)		−£884		−£12,580		+£15,100
DCF yield (ranking CAB)		12%		8.5%		15%

them by payback, rate of return, NPV and DCF yield methods.

The payback method selects project B as the most attractive investment but ignores the short life remaining after payback is completed. This is taken into account however by the DCF yield method which shows up project B in its true light as the least profitable of all three projects.

The rate of return method selects project A as the most profitable simply because the average profit per year is more than in the other two projects. When the timing of those profits is taken into account then project A is shown to give a DCF yield, or true return, of only 12% compared with its rate of return of 18%. Such inaccuracies have persuaded many firms to abandon the rate of return method and use the DCF yield method to appraise projects.

When project A is compared with project C on the DCF yield method the extra £8,000 profit on project A does not compensate for the slow build-up of the project. Even though total profit is £8,000 less on project C the project is more profitable than project A because discounting emphasizes the value of the earlier high returns.

In short, payback can yield useful information but must not be used by itself. Either discounting method will give more accurate results than the rate of return method when assessing the profitability of an investment over its whole life. Firms may sometimes calculate the rate of return expected in the first year of operation and compare this with the actual return earned for monitoring purposes. This monitoring or post-audit appraisal is an important part of project investment. However, the complexities of taxation, grants, working capital and other items reduce the validity of the rate of return method in many cases.

Ranking of projects

There are two ways to rank projects in order of attractiveness when using discounting techniques. The simplest is to rank them by the size of their DCF yields. When firms use only the NPV method the size of the NPV surplus is not related to the amount of capital invested to earn that surplus. To compare the relative profitability of projects on the NPV method we go a step further and calculate a profitability index by dividing the NPV inflow by the NPV outflow. Taking project C in figure 14.8 as an example the NPV inflows totalled £215,100 and the NPV outflow £200,000 giving a profitability index of 1.0755. Any project is viable when the profitability index exceeds 1.000 but its relative profitability against other projects can be measured by the size of the index number.

Care must be taken when ranking in the two special situations of capital rationing and the choice between alternative projects. The selection of projects when capital is insufficient must be based on the profitability index of the competing projects for those scarce funds. When a choice has to be made between alternative projects which are mutually exclusive it should be based on the highest NPV surplus.

Taxation

When appraising the worthwhileness of any investment in the private sector, the effects of tax must be taken into account. The payment of tax on profits is offset to some extent by tax allowances on certain new assets acquired. These tax transactions must be incorporated into the yearly cash flows after allowing for the time lag on the payment of tax. Tax allowances reduce the tax liability of the company as a whole, and are therefore subject to the same time lag as tax payments. The timing of tax payments and the size of tax allowances is explained in Chapter 18.

Let us take as an example a firm which buys a machine for

£100,000 which is expected to last four years. Taxable profits are estimated at £45,000 each year being sales less operating costs without charging depreciation. The firm pays tax at 35% and gets 25% per annum capital allowances on the machine on a reducing balance basis. The cash flows for this project can be set out as in figure 14.9 and discounted in the normal way.

Figure 14.9 Cash flows incorporating 35% tax

Year	Investment	Taxable profit	Tax paid at 35%	Capital allowance	Tax saved on allowance	Net cash flow
	£	£	£		£	£
0	−100,000					−100,000
1		+45,000		25,000		+ 45,000
2		+45,000	−15,750	18,750	+ 8,750	+ 38,000
3		+45,000	−15,750	14,063	+ 6,563	+ 35,813
4		+45,000	−15,750	42,187	+ 4,922	+ 34,172
5			−15,750		+14,765	− 985

Uncertainty

In most industrial investment appraisals there is no certainty that the eventual outcome will be exactly as predicted at the time of the appraisal. There are some crude methods we can use to minimize the risks involved. These methods include rejecting all projects which do not recover the initial investment in a specified number of years or varying the required rate of return according to how risky we view the project. Another method uses two further sets of cash flows based on optimistic and pessimistic assumptions. These set parameters within which we would expect to find the actual DCF yield.

More scientific methods can be used on important project appraisals where the capital to be spent is significant given the size of that particular company. Computers have an important contribution to make here when repetitive calculations are involved. One of these more sophisticated methods is to test the sensitivity of the return on investment to inaccuracies, or variations, in any one item of the cash flow whilst holding the other items constant.

Another method is to draw a decision tree which shows diagrammatically the various stages of a sequential decision process. Alternative courses of action open to the firm are depicted as branches of a tree and are assigned probability factors according to the likelihood of their occurrence. The value of each possible outcome is calculated by multiplying the benefit by its probability. The highest profit (or least cost) tells us which course of action to select.

Inflation

Up to this point the investment appraisal techniques discussed have implicitly ignored the existence of inflation and its effects on the future cash flows of projects being appraised.

Inflation brings additional problems to project appraisals. It increases the uncertainty and makes more difficult the estimation of the future cash flows including sales revenue, operating costs and working capital requirements. It also influences the required rate of return through its effects on the cost of capital.

In the context of investment appraisals it means that two aspects of the value of money must be considered. The time value of money has already been catered for by the use of present value factors which deduct interest for the time elapsed when waiting for future cash receipts. The other aspect is the change in the value of money itself, not because of the time lapse, but because the inflationary process decreases its purchasing power.

When describing how to allow for inflation in investment appraisals, and cope with both these aspects, it is useful first to distinguish between the real rate of return on a project and its nominal rate of return. A simple example may clarify this difference between real and nominal rates of return:

Suppose an investor receives an income of £100 p.a. on an investment of £1,000 then his nominal rate of return is 10%. If inflation is zero then his real rate of return will also be 10%. If, however, inflation is running at 6% per annum then his real rate of return is approximately the nominal rate minus the rate of inflation which leaves only 4%:

$$\text{real rate of return} \atop 0.04\,(4\%) = \left(\frac{\text{nominal rate of return } 1.10}{\text{rate of inflation } 1.06} \right) - 1$$

$$\text{or nominal rate of return} \atop 0.10\,(10\%) = \left(\text{real rate of return} \times \text{rate of inflation} \atop 1.04 \qquad\qquad 1.06 \right) - 1$$

Again, if inflation is running at 15% per annum then his nominal rate of return of 10% is swamped by inflation and he gets a negative real rate of return of about 5%. This experience was all too vivid for small investors in the 1970s when the rate of inflation frequently exceeded the rate of interest received on bank or building society deposits or other similar investments.

Turning to an industrial context a company's return on investment is the annual after-tax profit expressed as a percentage of the

146

capital employed in the business. This is a nominal rate of return. The real return on investment will be this nominal return less the rate of inflation and it should be recognized that the real rate of return for British industry generally has been less than 5% in many recent years.

The real and nominal rates of return referred to here for the whole company are not strictly correct because the concept of profit is not identical with that of cash flow. This is because profit ignores the timing of cash receipts and payments and can arise when cash is not even received. It is important to recognize that the company's one-year return on investment is conceptually different from the whole life project return based on the timing of cash flows. It is far from uncommon for a wholly satisfactory project with a high estimated return to have an adverse effect on the company profit and loss account, particularly in the first year or two. This is because the initial investment costs show as depreciation and interest charges before revenue starts to flow and profits are earned.

In the case of individual project appraisals the nominal rate of return is the apparent DCF yield found when discounting future cash flows that have been inflated to take account of anticipated inflation. The real rate of return on such a project however is this nominal rate of return minus the rate of inflation. If future cash flows on a project have been expressed in the constant value of Year 0 purchasing power then the solution DCF yield is the real rate of return.

At appraisal time we are therefore faced with a choice whether to express future cash flows at their inflated values and find the nominal rate of return or alternatively to express them in the constant purchasing power as at Year 0 and find the real rate of return. What influences us as to which choice to make depends on how top management express the target rate of return, and whether we see the future cash flows keeping pace with inflation or not. Most firms will probably express the target rate of return in nominal rather than real terms. This is because the target rate is often based on the nominal costs of borrowing or the opportunity cost of alternative financial investments.

Further reading

Investment Appraisal, Graham Mott, Pan.
Capital Investment and Financial Decisions, H. Levy and M. Sarnat, Prentice-Hall.

Self-check questions

1 What are the situations where an investment appraisal is relevant?
2 What is the payback period for the annual cash flows contained in figure 14.2?
3 What is the present value of £4,000 receivable in three years' time if the cost of capital is 12%?
4 What is the net present value of an investment of £20,000 now, with an annual cash return of £5,000 for ten years, if the cost of capital is 15%?
5 What is the DCF yield on the example in question 4?
6 Interpolate the DCF yield when the NPV surplus is £45,000 at 15% and the NPV deficit is £25,000 at 20%.
7 Is it worth buying a new machine costing £10,000 if it is expected to save £3,000 each year over a five-year life? The cost of capital is 14% and the company is not subject to corporation tax.
8 Differentiate between a 'real' and a 'nominal' rate of return.

15 Managing the working capital

The capital of a company is employed in two distinct areas. Some of it goes to provide the permanent or fixed assets like buildings, plant and vehicles. The remainder goes to provide the working capital necessitated by having to pay for the cost of goods and services before recovering the money from customers.

Figure 15.1 The employment of capital

Fixed assets
Buildings, plant, vehicles, etc.

Capital employed
Shareholders' funds, loans,
debentures, etc.

Working capital
Stocks, debtors, cash less creditors

Working capital is the value of all the current assets less the value of the current liabilities. It therefore includes the cost of stocks of raw materials, work-in-progress and finished goods together with the amount owed by customers less the amount owed to suppliers:

$$\boxed{\text{WORKING CAPITAL}} = \boxed{\text{STOCKS}} + \boxed{\text{DEBTORS}} + \boxed{\text{CASH}} - \boxed{\text{CREDITORS}}$$

The key to managing working capital successfully is to find the right balance between liquidity and profitability. A firm needs to be liquid enough to pay the wages and other bills when required, but on the other hand it needs to carry sufficient stocks so that production is not unduly disrupted nor customers dissatisfied with 'stock-outs'. Both these requirements can be met given unlimited working capital but much of it would be idle for long periods of time. This means that profit would be lost due to the extra holding costs of large stocks and the interest costs of the capital involved. Therefore we have to strike a balance between profitability and liquidity recognizing that they pull in opposite directions.

How much working capital is needed is obviously related to the volume of business, namely, the level of sales. If we divide the annual sales by the amount of working capital we find out how many times the working capital went round or circulated during the year.

For example, if sales last year were £2m and the average working capital was £0.5m then working capital circulated four times during the year. This circulation process is shown in figure 15.2.

Figure 15.2 The working capital cycle

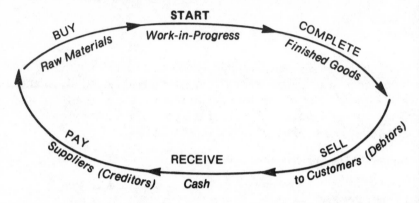

For an existing company we can find the working capital requirement from the relationship of working capital to sales. In the example mentioned above, working capital represented 25% of annual sales. Put another way, the firm needed 25p working capital for every £1 of sales. If this is typical of that firm's experience during the year and not an atypical year-end situation, we can say that for every £1 change in sales there will be a 25p change in working capital requirement. This may seem a crude relationship but it will give accurate enough results for some practical purposes.

Another way the working capital requirement can be determined is from the length of the 'operating cycle'. This term refers to the length of time between the company first paying out cash on materials, wages and overheads and the eventual receipt of cash from the sale of the goods or services produced. An example is given in figure 15.3 with hypothetical figures to illustrate the point.

Figure 15.3 Length of the operating cycle

	Weeks
Average time raw materials stay in stock	7
(−) Credit period granted by suppliers	(6)
	1
(+) Average time taken to produce the goods/services	3
(+) Average time finished goods stay in stock	2
(+) Average time customers take to pay	7
= Total length of operating cycle	13

Having determined the length of the operating cycle a firm can calculate the maximum working capital requirement from the sales forecast for that length of time. Using the above example of a thirteen-week cycle, if sales are forecast at £2m for the coming year, then £0.5m (i.e. $\frac{13}{52} \times £2m$) working capital will be required. This ignores the possibility of seasonal fluctuations when the £2m sales would not be evenly spread over the year. Similarly the working capital required will also fluctuate in advance of the fluctuation in the level of sales. Also ignored is the possibility of a change in stock levels.

The above calculation exaggerates due to the profit element in sales. Strictly speaking, the proportion $\frac{13}{52}$ should be applied to the cost of sales and not the full selling price.

A guide as to whether a firm has sufficient working capital and a viable mix of constituent items can be obtained from a look at two ratios previously met in Chapter 6.

The 'current ratio' of current assets to current liabilities looks for a norm of about 2:1, i.e. there should be £2 of current assets for every £1 of current liabilities. It may appear that this is an arbitrary figure but it has long been regarded by businessmen as reasonable. The premise is that half of the current assets are stocks and therefore not quickly turned into cash to pay the current liabilities.

Excluding stocks from current assets leaves us with liquid assets and here we look for the obvious 1:1 ratio. Notwithstanding, it is quite easy to find examples of companies operating quite successfully on ratios below this or below the 2:1 current ratio. One reason is that bank overdrafts are included in current liabilities but unless they are called in they are not a current liability in the normal sense of the word. Also firms may have unused overdraft facilities with which to counter an apparently unsatisfactory liquidity position.

In some particular industries it is quite usual to meet 'adverse' current ratios of less than 2:1 and this may be due to their individual circumstances. An example of this occurs in both food retailing and construction if stocks or work-in-progress are turned into cash before trade creditors have to be paid. In the past, supermarket operators have financed the acquisition of new premises from the credit obtained from food manufacturers, whose produce they have sold for cash before the manufacturers' invoices were due to be paid.

Having looked at working capital requirements in total, let us now examine how each constituent part is best managed.

The management of cash

There are two key instruments for managing cash – the cash budget and the statement of forecast sources and applications of funds. The former is the more detailed statement showing all the cash receipts and payments for the coming year broken down into monthly intervals. A typical example appears in figure 15.4 containing the cash transactions we might expect to find in a manufacturing business. The layout illustrated makes it easier to compile and ensures rapid assimilation of the information.

Figure 15.4 A cash budget for a manufacturing firm

Month	1	2	3	4	5	6	7	8	9	10	11	12
Cash inflows												
Sales												
Grant												
Total												
Cash outflows												
Wages												
Purchases												
Salaries												
Services												
Capital expenditure												
Tax												
Dividends												
Total												
Monthly+/–												
Cumulative+/–												

When compiling the cash budget it is essential to allow for the time lags on transactions. If a firm finds that credit customers take an average of eight weeks to settle their account, then sales that take place in month one will appear as a cash inflow in month three. Similarly, purchases will not be paid for in the month of purchase but in a later month depending on the credit period obtained from suppliers. Note also the absence of depreciation which is not a cash expense.

The other instrument which helps to manage cash is the forecast sources and applications of funds statement. It might be thought that this is similar to the cash budget but there are important distinctions. If we refer back to figure 7.2 in Chapter 7 it is clear that the sources and applications of funds statement is a summary of the detailed cash transactions. The first entry for example shows profit as a source of funds whereas a cash budget details the individual items of income and expenditure as they are paid for, not as they are incurred. The sources and applications of funds statement is therefore very useful in identifying the *causes* of the change in the liquid position. It highlights *changes* in the level of stocks and debtors, for example, which are not obvious from the cash budget which records the actual receipts and payments of cash.

Armed with these two statements we should now know the size, duration and causes of potential surpluses or deficits of cash. Short-term cash surpluses of a few months' duration should be invested short term to earn more profit, whilst being capable of being turned back into cash when required. Examples are the purchase of tax reserve certificates, Treasury bills or other short-dated government stocks or investment on the London money market. The taking of cash discounts for early payment to suppliers may be advisable if the annual rate of interest so earned exceeds that available on financial investments. If a surplus is disclosed that is expected to continue in later years, thought must be given to using this in the expansion or diversification of the existing business or in the acquisition of new businesses.

Forecast cash deficits obviously pose more of a problem than cash surpluses. A short-term deficit lasting only a few months will be disclosed in a cash budget and explained in the forecast sources and applications of funds. If the cause is a seasonal increase in stocks and debtors then the evidence of these statements will usually persuade the bank manager to extend overdraft facilities. Failing this, the firm may have to trim stocks, renegotiate credit terms, defer capital expenditure and somehow level-out the peak cash outflows.

Long-term cash deficits are caused by a move to an increased volume of business, large capital expenditure programmes or simply the effects of inflation which require more cash to finance the same activities. Such events have to be met by introducing new long-term capital. This may take the form of a rights issue of new shares or a loan or debenture repayable over a number of years or in a lump sum on redemption. Sale and leaseback of valuable premises may be a 'one-off' way of releasing funds for other uses but the rent will reduce profits in much the same way as would interest on a loan.

The management of debtors

Apart from retail shops, most UK companies sell on credit so their managers must decide who to sell to, on what terms and how to follow up late payments. When another firm applies for credit as a potential customer it would be rash indeed to agree credit without checking on credit worthiness. This can be done by employing a suitable agency like Dun & Bradstreet, or it can be carried out by the firm's own staff. Checks should include talking to other suppliers who have been quoted as trade references and checking bank references. Unfortunately the latter may say little more than the length of time the account has been operated. Sales representatives may form an opinion by calling at the potential client's premises and they may also hear valuable information on the informal grapevine. A copy of the client's annual accounts can be requested and perused using ratio analysis techniques to look at the profitability, liquidity and debt capacity. If an existing customer requests a higher credit limit, then his track record on prompt payment, or otherwise, can easily be checked.

Having decided who to sell to, a firm must now decide the terms of sale, being the length of the credit period and whether to offer cash discounts for early payment. The length of credit period is often settled by the normal terms for that particular industry. Firms compete with one another for custom and it would be difficult for one firm to impose a shorter credit period than its competitors, unless it had some compensating advantages. Typical credit terms demand payment by the end of the following month to that invoiced, which means between four and eight weeks' credit.

Cash discounts are a way of stimulating early payment, thereby reducing the amount of working capital required. The disadvantages lie in the cost and administrative burden. If a cash discount of 2% is offered for payment of invoice within two weeks, this may persuade customers to accept instead of taking a further four weeks' credit. A discount of 2% for four weeks is equivalent to an annual rate of 26%. If credit customers would have taken a further six weeks to pay after the expiry of the discount period then the 2% discount is equivalent to an annual rate of 17%.

Early payment induced by cash discounts will reduce profits but it may be largely compensated by not having to borrow so much capital. The effective annual rate of cash discounts can therefore be compared with the cost of bank overdrafts or loans, which would be

154

needed to finance the longer credit period taken when discounts are not offered.

The other factor to consider is administration and the loss of goodwill when disputes arise. Customers may claim cash discounts even though the cash is received after the end of the discount period. Sorting out this kind of problem can negate some of the advantages of early payment.

Some firms offer a tapering discount/penalty scheme where the cash discount reduces in steps as the normal credit period shortens, but after that a stepped penalty is added to the invoice value according to the lateness of payment. An example of this approach would be:

Payment within 2 weeks of invoice					3% discount	
"	"	4	"	"	"	2% "
"	"	6	"	"	"	1% "
Payment after	6	"	"	"	1% penalty
"	"	8	"	"	"	2% "

Having sold to credit customers and specified the payment terms we must consider what follow-up procedure to adopt with late payers. Many firms use a monthly statement, both as a reminder, and for the customer to check the balance on his account. If payment is not forthcoming in the stipulated time a reminder letter should be sent followed by a more strongly worded letter about a fortnight later. Should payment still not be received, consideration should be given to terminating supplies and instituting legal action and the customer informed accordingly.

Legal action for the recovery of the debt is appropriate where the debt is small or where the sale was subject to an unresolved dispute and the client's ability to pay is not in doubt. Where the debt is large and the customer's ability to pay is now in doubt, it may be more

Figure 15.5 Age analysis of debtors' invoices

Duration from invoice date	% of total debtors	Cumulative total %	Number of accounts
0–14 days	28%	28%	264
15–28 "	25%	53%	205
29–42 "	19%	72%	147
43–56 " Due date	14%	86%	82 Due date
57–70 "	7%	93%	38
71–84 "	4%	97%	16
85–98 "	2%	99%	20
99+ "	1%	100%	7

155

appropriate to bring matters to a head by applying to have the company wound up. A 'retention of title' clause may help to recover goods not yet paid for.

In this era of information technology, firms should have all the necessary information about customers' debts to hand. The overall debtor's position can be judged by the age analysis of invoices shown in figure 15.5. It can be seen that 14% of total debtors have exceeded the stipulated time allowed. Not all of this will be deliberate slow payment or potential bad debts, but will be partly caused by inflexible payment procedures in the client firms. This overdue proportion (14%) can be monitored against previous experience to identify trend movements and indicate a change in follow-up policy.

Apart from the overall debtors picture a print-out of individual overdue accounts is essential, with indicators of the follow-up stage reached in each case. Of particular concern will be the seven accounts which are more than three months old.

If an age analysis is not available, a rough guide to the credit period can be found by using the ratio $\frac{debtors}{sales} \times 365$ days, which will indicate the efficiency of credit control when compared with the period allowed.

The management of creditors

Trade creditors are debts owed to suppliers of goods and services in whose books they appear as debtors. The policy for dealing with creditors is very straightforward and mirrors that of debtors. If no cash discounts are offered then the full credit period should be taken. To do otherwise, by making an earlier payment, would reduce the profit by increasing the amount of working capital which had to be financed by borrowed capital with consequent interest payments.

If cash discounts are offered then the decision, like debtors, is whether the effective *annual* rate of interest earned by the discount exceeds the cost of capital used up by the early payment. Taking the example of a 2% cash discount for payment one month earlier than normally allowed, this equates to an annual rate of 24%. Provided the cost of available overdrafts, loans or other sources of capital is less than 24% it will be beneficial to take the cash discount.

An overall check on the period of credit taken can be found from the ratio relating trade creditors to purchases, namely

$\frac{\text{trade creditors}}{\text{purchases}} \times 365$ days. If creditors were £80,000 and the year's purchases £320,000 this equates to 91 days' credit taken from suppliers. This will serve as a reasonable guide provided the creditors figure is not abnormally high or low at this time.

The management of stocks

When looking at the current ratio we saw that the assumption is made that stocks represent half of current assets. There are three possible kinds of stocks – raw materials, work-in-progress and finished goods. In manufacturing industry all three types are likely to be present unless the product is to a customer's 'one-off' specification, when completed work is not usually held in stock. In service industries physical stocks are not so prevalent but work-in-progress in the form of wages, salaries and overheads may be very significant. Architects, for example, are rewarded pro rata to the value of building work done, but many months of work are put in at the design stage when no money is received from clients.

In an ideal situation firms would need no stocks. Raw materials would be delivered daily; production would be completed the same day and the finished goods would immediately be sold and delivered to customers. This situation is most unusual in practice because firms buy in bulk to reduce the unit cost of purchases and to hold some stock as an insurance against non-delivery. Production is not completed the same day in some industries. In many cases work-in-progress may consist of a number of stages when the need for buffer stocks and economical production runs leads to an abundance of components. Diverse product ranges result in larger stocks of work-in-progress and finished goods than found in a single product company.

To ensure that production is never halted for lack of materials or component parts, and that customers are never dissatisfied, might entail holding very large stocks. The working capital tied up in this way ensures that firms produce and sell efficiently, but profits are offset by the costs of warehousing, possible deterioration and, most significantly, the interest on the capital tied up in stocks.

Managing stocks requires balancing these conflicting factors. It means setting stock levels to allow for normal delivery times plus a small buffer stock for safety. This is achieved by calculating the reorder level which on normal usage will reduce the buffer stock level by the time delivery has been achieved. For example, if a firm uses 200 kg of material 'X' per week and delivery takes three weeks then the reorder level will be the buffer stock plus 600 kg. The other balancing act occurs when setting the economic order quantity (EOQ). When buying in large quantities, extra discounts and reduced ordering and handling costs will be achieved, but these advantages are offset by the increased interest and storage costs. Conversely, if frequent orders are placed, interest and storage costs will be reduced but ordering, handling and the unit purchase cost will increase. A formula is available for solving EOQ where

A = annual usage in units,
S = ordering/handling cost per order,
i = cost of carrying stock as a %,
C = unit cost of the stock item:

$$EOQ = \sqrt{(2AS/iC)}$$

Sometimes firms have to cut their cloth according to the finance available for stocks. Many firms these days simply cannot afford stock levels which ensure continuous production in large runs or 100% customer satisfaction. This is the reason for the move towards 'just-in-time' ordering systems, which, as the name implies, means holding little in the way of buffer stocks and passes the stockholding costs on to the supplier.

Material requirements planning

The above formula for EOQ assumes demand is reasonably constant whereas in fact it may fluctuate considerably. This means that stock levels are much higher than they need be for considerable periods of time. Instead of estimating demand from past experience, material requirements planning is based on what needs to be purchased or manufactured to fulfill the planned level of production, to meet actual or expected orders from customers. The demand for components to satisfy production needs is reduced by the stock-in-hand, and the net balance, when compared with the supply picture, determines when to initiate the order. Unwanted stock is not kept for long periods under this MRP system and the reduction in finance, storage and obsolescence costs can be considerable. Computers make the operation of this system feasible even when large numbers of components are involved.

Further reading

Management of Company Finance, J. M. Samuels and F. M. Wilkes, Van Nostrand Reinhold.
Control of Working Capital, M. Grass, Gower.

Self-check questions

1 Define 'working capital'.
2 How can a firm determine the extra working capital required if sales are expected to increase by £100,000 next month and stay at that level?
3 Draw a pro forma cash budget for the firm of your choice using the layout in figure 15.4.
4 What checks would you undertake before granting credit to a new trade customer?
5 What is the annual cost of granting cash discounts of 2% if it results in payment five weeks earlier?
6 How many days credit are being taken by customers when debtors are £57,000 and annual sales are £250,000? Ignore seasonal fluctuations.
7 Name the three possible kinds of stock.
8 What decisions do firms have to take to ensure they do not run out of stocks of materials?

16 Share values

Share capital is provided by the owners of limited companies and therefore relates to the private sector, apart from odd exceptions like BL placed somewhere between public and private sectors. We saw in Chapter 4 that there are two main types of shares – preference shares and ordinary shares. Preference shares carry the right to a fixed rate of dividend before ordinary shareholders receive any dividend. Usually preference shareholders have no further right to an increased dividend, irrespective of the level of profit attained by their company.

Value of preference shares

The value of preference shares is therefore dependent on the rate of dividend attached to those shares and its relationship with the rate currently offered on new shares. Where there is a risk of non-payment of dividend it will depress the market price of the shares. This will be very marked if the situation is expected to last some years and the arrears of dividend are not allowed to be accumulated over this period.

Ignoring the possibility of non-payment let us take as an example the 7% £1 preference shares in XYZ Ltd when the current rate of dividend being offered on similar new shares is 10%. Obviously no one will pay £1 for existing shares giving them a 7% return when they can buy new shares offering a 10% return. The price of the 7% shares will fall to a level where the holder receives a 10% return.

$$\text{Preference share value} = £1 \times \frac{7\%}{10\%} = 70\text{p}$$

Where special voting rights attach to preference shares or where repayment is drawing close then the share price will reflect these factors. For tax reasons mentioned earlier, preference shares are now uncommon and our main concern is with the value of a company's ordinary shares.

Value of ordinary shares

There are a number of possible reasons why ordinary shares need to be valued. When a public limited company first offers its shares to the public it needs to fix a price at a small discount to what the shares are thought to be worth. If a company is taken over its shares are bought by another company, or an individual, and those shares have to be valued to fix the cash purchase price or the value of any shares issued in exchange.

There are two taxes relating to the wealth owned by individuals. *Capital gains tax* applies to profits on the sale of shares, whilst *inheritance tax* applies to the value of shares given or bequeathed to another person. Normally the relevant value is the stock market price at the time of sale or transfer. In the case of private limited companies which are debarred from a stock market quotation, some other means of valuing shares has to be found.

There are two main approaches to valuing ordinary shares. We can either value them according to the assets they own or according to the profits earned on those assets.

Assets basis of valuation

Let us take as an example EZ Engineering Ltd whose balance sheet reads:

		£000			£000
£1 Ordinary shares		500	*Fixed assets*		
Revenue reserves		450	Land and buildings		350
		——	Machinery, vehicles, etc.		700
Shareholders' funds		950			——
Loans		425			1,050
			Current assets		
Current liabilities			Stocks, work-		
Trade creditors	150		in-progress	400	
Bank overdraft	175	325	Debtors	250	650
	——	——		——	——
		1,700			1,700
		═══			═══

The value of the assets owned by ordinary shareholders is the value of total assets (£1.7m) less total debts to outsiders (£0.75m), making £0.95m. This is of course the same as the value of shareholders' funds which represent the net worth or the equity. The asset value per share is the value of shareholders' funds or assets belonging to shareholders, divided by the number of shares issued:

$$\text{asset value} = \frac{\text{shareholders' funds}}{\text{number of shares}} = \frac{£950,000}{500,000} = £1.90 \text{ per share.}$$

This £1.90 value is referred to as 'book value' because it is based on the balance sheet value of the assets. If the assets are valued at their current worth to the company as a 'going concern', this may lead to a different value of the shares. Suppose the land and buildings in EZ Engineering's balance sheet have just been professionally valued at £550,000. This increases the value of the shareholders' funds by £200,000 and consequently the individual share value to £2.30 on a going concern basis.

Goodwill

When a company buys out another company it takes over the physical assets and debts of that other company. In addition, it takes over the established name of the company which has been built up over a long period of time. The value of that name and reputation is an intangible asset and is known as 'goodwill'. Most companies have their own goodwill but it is an impossible thing to value as we cannot say what specific amount has been spent on its creation.

Goodwill only appears in a balance sheet when it literally has been bought off another company. Usually this is done by taking over another company and paying more for the shares than the value of the physical assets acquired, less any debts assumed. The excess represents the payment for goodwill. In the case of EZ Engineering, £2.30 per share represents the current value of assets owned by shareholders. Assuming EZ's shareholders were paid £2.50 on a takeover, then the purchaser has paid £100,000 (i.e. 20p×500,000) for goodwill.

If a company has gone into liquidation it may be possible to buy only the trade name from the liquidator, without taking over any physical assets. In this situation the whole payment represents the cost of goodwill.

Sometimes goodwill is calculated as X number of years purchase of profits. This is not a scientific calculation so much as an attempt to measure the purchase cost of goodwill against the annual profit achieved. In the final analysis, goodwill is worth only the discounted future benefits accruing to the name and reputation acquired.

Even when companies pay out money for goodwill it does not

always appear in their balance sheet. This is because companies often take the earliest opportunity to 'write it off'. This is similar to the depreciation process when an asset is reduced in value in the balance sheet by transferring some of its cost to the profit and loss account. It is not normally included in the list of trading expenses but shown as an exceptional item below the line where the normal trading profit is determined.

Earnings basis of valuation

The second main approach to valuing ordinary shares is based on the profit after tax attributable to each share. Such profit is referred to as the 'earnings per share' and represents the total profit (after charging interest, tax and preference dividends) divided by the number of ordinary shares:

$$\text{earnings per share} = \frac{\text{profit attributable to ordinary shareholders}}{\text{number of ordinary shares}}$$

In the case of EZ Engineering there were 500,000 £1 ordinary shares in existence. Let us assume that the profit after tax was £150,000, in which case:

$$\text{earnings per share} = \frac{£150,000}{500,000} = 30p$$

An earnings per share calculated from last year's profit may not be a good guide to the future maintainable profit if last year was in any way abnormal. Companies do occasionally make an annual loss in which case the earnings per share is negative. In both situations an estimate is needed of the future profit and hence the earnings per share that can be achieved in the coming year(s).

Assuming we know the earning per share, this is translated into a share value by using a comparative price/earnings (p/e) ratio for other companies in the same field. A p/e ratio relates the earnings per share to the market value of the share as follows:

$$\text{price/earnings ratio} = \frac{\text{market price of the share}}{\text{earnings per share}}$$

In the case of p.l.c.'s with a Stock Exchange quotation these p/e ratios can be found in the financial press or calculated from the company's accounts using the current market price. With unlisted or private companies this market price is non-existent. A merchant bank or trade association can sometimes be approached to advise on a comparative p/e ratio for companies in the same industry with a similar profit record and prospects.

Referring back to EZ Engineering Ltd we assumed that its earnings per share was 30p. If we now assume that similar small engineering companies have a p/e ratio of about 5 we can derive the share value for EZ Engineering by multiplying the earnings per share by this comparative ratio:

$$\text{share value}=30\text{p}\times5=\pounds1.50$$

This is a smaller value than that obtained on the assets basis (£2.30) for the same company but it would be sheer coincidence if they were identical. This is because share prices tend to fluctuate from day to day, so therefore must the p/e ratios as the earnings per share is a constant figure until the next year's profit is known. Share prices based on earnings can also be higher than asset value, particularly in service industries where profits are more related to the skills of employees than the use of assets.

An examination of p/e ratios in, say, the *Financial Times*, will reveal wide disparities between apparently similar companies operating in the same industry. A favourite example of mine is to compare Marks & Spencer with Woolworths. Both companies operate in the main town centres offering a broadly similar range of products. During the 1970s Marks & Spencer achieved a growth of sales, profits and dividends well in excess of Woolworths and most other stores. Consequently its shares were more highly regarded by investors who were willing to buy at a market price reflecting a much higher p/e ratio than they were prepared to pay for Woolworths shares. Investors clearly expected that increased profits in future years would soon bring the p/e ratio down if calculated on the market price at the time of their original purchase.

Another reason why a p/e ratio may appear abnormal in comparison with other companies is when it is calculated on historic earnings per share, which are not expected to be maintained. A company can experience internal problems peculiar to itself, for example a strike. On the other hand, it may be about to launch a new product, as in the case of drug manufacturers whose share prices are very sensitive to new product announcements even though they may take some years to filter through into actual earnings. Rumours of an impending takeover may be another reason for an apparently high p/e ratio if earnings on assets are poor and the asset value per share considerably higher than the value based on earnings alone.

Discounted earnings basis of valuation

A theoretically sound approach to valuing ordinary shares is to calculate the present value of the stream of future earnings going on to perpetuity. This present value approach progressively reduces the worth of future earnings by deducting compound interest for the waiting time, as explained in Chapter 14. The sum of the present value for each year represents the current value of the shares. For any one firm the discount rate used will be its cost of capital, whilst for an individual it will be the opportunity cost of the return available on alternative investments. Although useful for valuing securities with a fixed rate of return, it is not so easy in practice to estimate future earnings on ordinary shares for most companies.

Stock Exchange

The Stock Exchange is a market where financial securities are bought and sold and where, like any other market, the forces of supply and demand determine prices. There are markets in government stocks and foreign stocks and shares, in addition to the UK company stocks and shares which are our main concern.

The existence of the Stock Exchange allows companies to tap a wide body of investors. It also allows those investors the means to realize their capital at any time by selling their shares to someone else through the market, without the company being involved. These transactions in second-hand shares form the bulk of the activity in the market.

Another function of the Stock Exchange is as a barometer of business confidence through the movement of share prices. Various indices of share prices are available, the most famous being the *Financial Times* 'industrial ordinary share index' of thirty leading companies. Less well known, but more representative of price movements, is the 'all share index' of five hundred large companies which is not restricted to industrial concerns.

Jobbers and brokers

There are two distinct types of member of the Stock Exchange. Jobbers are the actual dealers in stocks and shares and quote two prices without knowing if the transaction will be a purchase or sale. The higher is their selling price and the lower is their buying price with the difference representing their profit margin or 'turn'. They adjust these prices according to how many shares they hold as well as in anticipation of market movements.

Investors cannot approach a jobber direct but must deal through a broker. He acts as their agent and tries to negotiate the best deal by inquiring prices from more than one jobber before finalizing a deal. At the end of 1986 the so called 'Big Bang' ended this strict separation of the roles of brokers and market makers, the latter term now being used in place of jobbers. Big Bang also allowed financial institutions like banks to own Stock Exchange subsidiaries and abolished the system of fixed commission rates.

Fluctuations in share prices

It should be noted that share prices reflect future expectations rather than current or past performance, with many investors looking up to a year ahead. Many factors influence share prices by working on the levels of supply and demand. General factors which affect share prices across the board are announcements of economic indicators, possible changes in government, wars, strikes and even international events. More specific factors affecting the share price of only one company are announcements (or rumours) regarding profits, dividends, orders, changes in management, new share issues and other happenings.

When a company announces its interim or final profit and dividend, there may not be any change in the share price, even when the figures are significantly different from the previous year. Only if the announcement is different to that expected, and already discounted in the share price, will there be any further price movement.

New issues

Invariably limited companies start off as private companies and gradually grow in size. A company goes public and gets a listing on the Stock Exchange when its capital needs are no longer met internally, when the owners wish to realize some of their investment or get a value for tax purposes.

Both a merchant bank (issuing house) and a stockbroker are

appointed to the company to help guide it through the lengthy process and value the shares at a realistic level. The price is fixed at the last possible minute to take account of the p/e ratios of similar companies and market conditions at the time. Underwriters agree to take up any unwanted shares for a small commission and this ensures the success of the venture whatever the market conditions on the day.

Very large companies that are already household names may succeed in going public by issuing a 'prospectus' and inviting investors to subscribe. These cases are very rare. More usually a company sells the shares to a merchant bank which in turn offers them to the investing public at a slightly higher price. This 'offer for sale' may be composed partly of new shares to raise capital for the company, and partly of existing shares where the original shareholders wish to realize some of their capital.

Small companies can avoid some of the advertising and other expenses by obtaining Stock Exchange permission for a 'placing'. Instead of offering shares to the general public by an offer for sale, shares are placed initially with clients of the broker and merchant bank handling the issue. Occasionally one hears of an 'introduction' when a company with a large number of existing shareholders, or with a listing abroad, gets a quotation on the London Stock Exchange. No new shares are involved necessarily, but sufficient shares must be made available to the jobbers to allow the market to function.

Offer by tender

When fixing the price of shares for an offer for sale or placing, account will be taken of the standing of similar companies with regard to financial yardsticks such as p/e ratio, dividend yield and dividend cover. Occasionally a company comes to the market which is rather unique in the sense that no other companies in the same field already have a quotation. Such a company is a suitable candidate for the 'tender' approach. When the government privatized Amersham in 1981 it offered the shares at a fixed price, but considerably underestimated the substantial premium that investors were willing to pay for such a high-technology company. Attempts were made to persuade the government that any future issues would use the tender method but this was not implemented until 1987 with the partial tender offer for British Airports.

When an offer for sale is by tender, applications are invited from investors at or above a stated minimum price. All shares are eventually issued at the same striking price which represents the lowest price at which the last shares on offer are taken up. Those investors who are very keen to buy will offer a very high price hoping this will secure an allocation of shares at a lower striking price. Let us assume that Company X offers 500,000 shares for sale at a minimum price of £2 each and gets the following tender bids:

Number of shares	Tender price
7,500,000	£2.00
1,350,000	£2.10
625,000	£2.20
300,000	£2.30
125,000	£2.40
50,000	£2.50
25,000	£2.80

Ignoring the possibility of large applicants being scaled down, the striking price would be fixed at £2.30, being the highest price at which all 500,000 shares can be sold. Applicants who tendered less than £2.30 would receive no shares.

Rights issues

Companies with an existing stock market quotation also issue new shares. When they issue them for cash it is known as a 'rights' issue, whereas when they are 'free' it is called a 'scrip' issue. It is important to understand the reasons for these issues and the effect on the share price of the company concerned.

The simplest to understand is a rights issue, when a company raises more capital either to finance its assets or to repay borrowed capital and so reduce its gearing. Existing shareholders are first given the right to buy the new shares pro rata to the number of shares they already own. For example they may be offered a 1 for 5 at £1.50 which means they can buy one new share at £1.50 for every five they already hold.

When a rights issue is first announced it may have a depressing effect on the existing share price. This is partly because of the threat of a larger than normal number of shares coming on to the market, due to some existing shareholders being unwilling or unable to put up more money. It is also a response to the size of the discount offered by the company, as the new shares will be offered at a price at least 10% lower than the market price to ensure the success of the issue.

After the rights issue has been effected the market price can be estimated from the following formula:

$$\text{ex-rights price} = \text{subscription price} + \left(\text{£ discount} \times \frac{\text{number of shares pre issue}}{\text{number of shares post issue}} \right)$$

In the case of the 1 for 5 issue at £1.50 previously mentioned let us assume the market price stood at £1.74 before the issue was announced. After the issue the share price should be:

$$\text{£1.50} + \left(24p \times \frac{5}{6} \right) = \text{£1.70}$$

Very often share prices may not conform with the above pattern. This is possibly because at the time of the issue the company makes an updated forecast of future profits and dividends. If this is better, or worse, than market expectations then the share price will move accordingly.

Shareholders who do not wish to excercise their rights can sell them in the market provided the subscription price is less than the current market price. To reduce expenses for small investors, the company sometimes does this on their behalf after the expiry date.

Scrip issues

A scrip issue is a very different animal. Here the company issues new shares to existing shareholders on a pro rata basis, but receives no cash for them. The mechanism of a scrip issue is to capitalize reserves, meaning that the issued share capital is increased whilst the reserves are decreased by the same amount. This is merely a book entry and may be thought of little purpose.

There are a number of reasons why scrip issues occur. A creditor or banker may insist on it as a safeguard to his interests. Certain reserves can be used for dividend payments if cash is available and this could be at the expense of creditors who are owed money. Once reserves are made up into share capital, dividends can no longer be paid from this source.

Companies usually express dividends as X pence per share as opposed to the previous practice of declaring them as a percentage of the par value of a share. This can be misleading for employees in particular, who may not see that the dividend is a return on all shareholders' funds and not just the issued capital. Very often scrip issues are a public relations exercise with employees and share-holders, based on their inadequate knowledge of company finance.

Small investors prefer low-priced shares to high-priced ones for psychological reasons. A £10 share is really just as valuable as ten £1 shares. Scrip issues have the effect of lowering the market price of a share pro rata to the size of the issue. Say, for example, a 1 for 1 scrip issue is made then the market price of shares should halve. If a 1 for 2 issue is made then the price should fall by one-third leaving the investor no better and no worse off. Take two shares which stand at £3 each before a 1 for 2 scrip issue. After the issue a shareholder will still hold £6 (3×£2) value as he did before.

As with rights issues the share price may not respond as described if a dividend forecast accompanying the scrip issue does not equate with market expectations.

Dividend cover

We saw with preference shares that the market price was based on the size of the dividend payment. This is not the case with ordinary shares because very few companies pay out all their profit as dividends. A combination of inflation and growth means that firms need extra capital each year to finance the increased value of fixed assets and working capital. The prime source of this extra capital is retained profit.

The proportion of profit paid out as dividend is ascertained from the 'dividend cover' expressed as:

$$\text{dividend cover} = \frac{\text{earnings per share}}{\text{dividend per share}}$$

Because of complications with irrecoverable advance corpora-tion tax and overseas taxation there is more than one method of calculation of dividend cover. In essence, where earnings per share is 21p and the net dividend is 7p the dividend cover is three times meaning that one-third of the profit is paid out as dividends:

$$\frac{21p}{7p} = 3.0 \text{ times}$$

This financial ratio is used as a measure of risk to the dividend should profits decline in future years. It is also used to express the proportion of earnings retained, in this case two-thirds.

Dividend yield

The dividend yield is the gross dividend expressed as a percentage of the current market price. Dividends are paid net by companies, as the advance corporation tax also satisfies the standard rate of income tax for the shareholder. Dividend yields are usually measured gross because any individual's tax liability is unknown, and also because the return offered on most other alternative investments is also expressed in gross terms.

In the above example of a 7p net dividend this is equivalent to a 10p gross dividend with the standard rate of tax at 30% ($7p \times \frac{100}{70} = 10p$). If the market price of the share is £1.60 then:

$$\text{Gross dividend yield} = \frac{10p}{160p} \times \frac{100}{1}\% = 6.25\%$$

This can now be compared with returns on other investments or other shares. It must be remembered that dividends are only part of the return received by investors. This is because retained profits are also expected to increase the market price of the shares over time. For this reason ordinary shares can not be valued by reference to their dividend yield. All earnings should be taken into account irrespective of whether they are retained or distributed as dividends. A more valid approach is to use the comparative p/e ratio mentioned earlier to value ordinary shares.

Dividend policy

In the case of small private companies the shareholders are usually either directors or members of their families. The dividend policy of these companies takes into account the need to retain profits as additional capital, as well as considering the needs and tax status of the shareholders regarding dividend income.

Public companies with a stock market quotation must consider their shareholders when framing their dividend policy. We have seen that the dividend yield at any moment in time is not a means to valuing shares. Shareholders do expect their company to pursue a consistent dividend policy and not use retained profits as the sole source of new finance. Should a company have pursued a policy, say, of distributing one half of its profit over a number of years, then this policy will be expected to continue. Any reduction of dividends to fund high capital expenditure will be greeted by a sharp fall in the market value of the shares. Although this does not immediately have any effect on the company, it makes future 'rights' issues more difficult and could lead to a takeover bid.

Further reading

Business Finance, F. W. Paish and R. J. Briston, Pitman.
Management of Company Finance, J. M. Samuels and F. M. Wilkes, Van Nostrand Reinhold.
Theory and Practice of Investment, T. G. Goff, Heinemann.

Self-check questions

1 What is the market value of a non-redeemable 11% preference share of £1 if the current rate of dividend on new shares is 9%?
2 What are the advantages and disadvantages to an investor of holding preference shares?
3 What are the three main ways of valuing ordinary shares?
4 What is goodwill?
5 Takeover activity often increases at times when share prices are high. Why is this so?
6 Differentiate between market makers and brokers.
7 Name the different ways a new issue can come to the market.
8 Why do shares often fall in value when a 'rights' issue is announced?
9 Why do companies make 'scrip' issues?
10 Define 'dividend cover'.
11 What is the dividend yield on a share with a market value of £1.60 when the net dividend is 9p and advance corporation tax is 30%?

17 Mergers, takeovers and buy-outs

The terminology used in this connection is not as precise as first appearances might suggest. A merger is when two or more companies join together voluntarily under the umbrella of a newly formed holding company. The parties concerned have equal status in the discussions leading up to the merger even when the companies involved are unequal in size.

A takeover is when one company buys out the shareholders in another company. It implies the unwillingness of one party and the use of force by the other. Very often this is not the case, as with an 'agreed takeover'. This represents a merger in many ways, except that no new holding company is formed and the larger company buys the issued shares of the smaller company. Should the smaller company take over the larger company, this is known as a 'reverse takeover'.

In recent years 'buy-outs' have become more frequent. When a particular activity no longer fits into the corporate plan of a holding company, it may decide to divest itself of that subsidiary. Sometimes group overheads charged to the subsidiary result in an inadequate return on capital. Occasionally companies go into receivership with potentially profitable activities submerged by other loss-making subsidiaries. All of these situations yield potential candidates for a buy-out by their management and other employees.

In the case of mergers and takeovers the reasons are somewhat different to those of management buy-outs. Any amalgamation should fit in with the corporate strategy of the principal company involved. The purpose is to make the combined companies more profitable, and stronger, than was the sum of their separate parts.

Very often economies of scale are cited as the justification for mergers and takeovers. These are described as technical, financial, marketing, managerial and risk-bearing economies resulting from the integration of activities.

Integration can take three forms – vertical, horizontal and lateral.

Vertical integration occurs when two companies at different stages join together under common ownership. A company can integrate forward to the market outlets or backward to the raw material and component supplies. An example of forward vertical integration is a shoe manufacturer taking over a chain of shoe shops, whilst a manufacturer taking over a leather tannery represents backward vertical integration. The main economies will be financial, resulting from the coordination of production and marketing functions and the elimination of middlemen profits.

Horizontal integration occurs when two companies at the same stage combine together. The purpose may be to eliminate competition or to broaden the product range and geographical coverage. Many economies are possible in this situation including technical, marketing, managerial and financial benefits.

Lateral integration is the third possibility, being a diversification from existing activities as when a construction company buys a shipping company. An attraction here could be if the particular industrial cycles do not coincide, so that risks are spread.

Occasionally a financial economy occurs through the workings of our tax system. If one company has accumulated tax losses or unclaimed capital allowances it may be possible for them to be offset against profits of another company. Although Chancellors have tightened up the rules over the years, losses can be worth taking over and may be the main attraction to a predator.

Asset-stripping days seem to be behind us, but there will always be opportunist bids where a company appears to be lowly valued in the market. This may follow a particularly bad set of annual results or may be the result of years of poor management. New owners may be willing to take a long hard look at the component parts, weeding out unprofitable or misplaced activities. Money raised from such divestments, or from the sale and leaseback of properties, may go some way to funding the original purchase price.

Another reason for amalgamations of companies may be the need for management succession. Where the founder owners of a private company have no suitable successors within the family, they may seek a merger or takeover with a larger public company to safeguard their investment.

Valuation of a business

Control of a business rests with shareholders who own the voting shares. Where voting powers are vested in the ordinary shares the value of a business is the total value of these shares. Occasionally, voting rights are vested in preference or other special categories of ordinary shares, but these are rare occurrences.

In the previous chapter we saw that there are the following different approaches to valuing ordinary shares:

- *Asset value.* Each share is represented by a proportionate part of the assets owned by the company after allowing for the payment of all debts. If we value these net assets and divide by the number of issued ordinary shares we arrive at the asset value per share. An additional amount may be added for goodwill as discussed previously.

- *Earnings value.* The earnings per share is the amount of profit earned for each ordinary share after tax, interest and preference dividends have been allowed. We try to find comparable companies and use their price/earnings ratio as a basis for valuing the shares of the company in question.

- *Stock market value.* This value is relevant in mergers and takeovers in the case of a public limited company with a quotation on the Stock Exchange. Very few bids succeed at the existing stock market price unless it has been pushed too high on takeover rumours, or major shareholders agree to sell at a lower price. A higher price than the pre-bid stock market value is needed because market prices are based on willing buyers and sellers at the margin. To tempt all existing shareholders to sell their shares may require substantially higher prices and 20–50% premiums are not uncommon.

Tactics

The price a bidder is prepared to pay for another company depends on a number of factors. Obviously an assessment of the asset value and earnings value can be made bearing in mind the broad changes that the new management propose. As previously mentioned, no bid is likely to succeed at a price below stock market value where this exists. Any additional payment for goodwill over and above tangible asset value depends on the reason for the bid and the strengths of the two parties.

Tactics are not very relevant in a merger where the good faith of both companies' management is paramount. In a takeover, particularly if it is opposed, battle lines are drawn very much as in chess. Each side proceeds with caution, one move at a time, anticipating and countering the other side's move.

The bidder usually tries to gain a foothold by acquiring himself, or through associates, a stake in the other company. If this is done through normal market purchases the effect on the other company's share price may lead to speculation of an impending bid. This can be avoided by spreading such purchases over a long period of time but it is not possible to build up a large stake secretly due to preventive measures in the City Takeover Code.

Defending an unwanted bid depends on that management's record and the proportion of total shares under their control. If the company has just announced poor results and the directors own only a tiny proportion of the total issued shares then any price significantly above the present market price will be hard to resist. On the other hand a company with a good track record of profit and dividend growth, together with a substantial director interest in the shares, may be able to fight off an unwelcome bid or demand such a high price that the bidder withdraws.

Very few bids are either successful at the first attempt or withdrawn on first refusal. Sometimes three or four increased bids are made in response to the defending management's arguments, all of which are given space in the national financial press as well as being mailed personally to each shareholder. Once 90% acceptance of a bid has been achieved the remaining 10% can be compulsorily acquired at the same price. Even when 90% acceptance is not achieved, but voting control passes to the predator, the remaining minority shareholders should think their position over carefully. There is no guarantee that the new parent will follow dividend policies to their liking and it may be wiser to accept the bid rather than be 'locked in' without an effective voice.

Monopolies Commission

Mergers and takeovers are not allowed to take place without due regard to the public interest, particularly where a reduction in competition would result from the proposed amalgamation of companies. In cases where substantial assets are to be acquired, or where a monopoly of more than one third of the market would result, the Department of Industry can refer the proposal to the Monopolies Commission. Such a reference can effectively kill off a proposal as the necessary investigations may take up to six months and the resulting uncertainty causes difficulty in share dealings of the companies involved.

Not all proposed amalgamations are referred in this way and there have been many instances of governments actively promoting mergers in a bid to strengthen home industries and fight off foreign competition. British Leyland is a case in point when the successful Leyland Motor Company was persuaded to take over the less successful British Motor Corporation with the promise of financial assistance.

Consideration

This refers to the form in which the purchase price is paid. Possible types of consideration are ordinary or preference shares, loan stock or cash itself. Only cash counts as a disposal for capital gains tax purposes and this may prove unpopular with large shareholders to whom it would apply. Gains of several thousand pounds are exempt in any tax year so small shareholders are not influenced in the same way.

Payment can be effected in preference shares or loan stock, both of which have a fixed rate of return. These will not be so popular with the ordinary shareholders being bought out, as their investment requirements are usually growth of dividend income and an increasing value of their capital. Neither preference shares nor loan stock participate in the changing prosperity of the parent company but they do enhance the gearing benefits for the latter company's ordinary shareholders.

A compromise often reached is to offer a mixture of securities and cash in exchange for the shares in the recipient company. Another alternative is to offer to pay in convertible loan stock. This starts its life as a conventional loan with a fixed rate of interest but carries the right to be converted into a predetermined number of ordinary shares in the parent company at a future date. From the bidders' point of view no dilution of equity is involved immediately, and a lower rate of interest can be offered than that acceptable on a pure loan stock. When conversion takes place at a future date it is anticipated that earnings from the company taken over will have grown sufficiently to offset any dilution of equity earnings in the parent company.

Sometimes the management of the two companies cannot agree on the value of the one to be taken over because of uncertainty as to the level of its future profits. This situation can be resolved by the offer of a performance related purchase price when the initial down-payment is supplemented by later additional payments on achievement of agreed profit targets.

The following short case study illustrates the valuation of a company's shares in an agreed takeover context.

Example

A large public company has just been approached by the directors of EZ Engineering Ltd (a smaller private company) with a view to merging the two companies. The latest balance sheet of EZ Engineering Ltd showed:

Balance sheet as at 31 December 19X4				
Liabilities		£000	Assets	£000
£1 ordinary shares		500	Fixed assets	
Revenue reserves		350	Freehold land and buildings	
6% debentures (redeemable Jan.			(at cost)	350
19X6)		400	Plant and machinery (net)	600
Current liabilities			Vehicles, etc. (net)	100
Creditors	150			1,050
Bank overdraft	175			
Tax payable	125	450	Current assets	
			Stock and work-	
			in-progress	400
			Debtors	250	650
		£1,700		£1,700

The directors of EZ Engineering Ltd have also disclosed the following information:

(a) On a going concern basis the values of assets and current liabilities are all reasonable except that a recent professional valuation puts the freehold land and buildings at £550,000.

(b) In a liquidation, stock and work-in-progress would fetch only about £250,000 and redundancies would cost another £250,000.

(c) After-tax profits have been static in real terms over the last three years, being £150,000 in 19X4 and this level is expected to -be maintained. The pretax figure was £275,000 and a normal return would be 20% on total assets.

(d) Public companies of a similar size to EZ Engineering Ltd have been averaging price/earnings ratios of 5 recently on the London Stock Exchange.

Calculate and discuss the various methods of valuing the ordinary shares of EZ Engineering Ltd on the basis that its directors are willing sellers, and state reasons for the valuation you think most reasonable to both parties.

Calculation of value of ordinary shares

	Book value	Break-up value	Going concern value
A Asset basis			
	£	£	£
Fixed assets	1,050,000	1,250,000	1,250,000
Current assets	650,000	500,000	650,000
	1,700,000	1,750,000	1,900,000
Current liabilities	450,000	450,000	450,000
	1,250,000	1,300,000	1,450,000
Debentures	400,000	400,000	400,000
	850,000	900,000	1,050,000
Redundancy costs	—	250,000	—
Value of assets owned by ordinary shareholders	£850,000	£650,000	£1,050,000
Number of ordinary shares	500,000	500,000	500,000
Value per share	£1.70	£1.30	£2.10

B Earnings basis	
Maintainable annual profit after tax	£150,000
Number of ordinary shares	500,000
Earnings per share	30p
Comparative price/earnings ratio	5
Value per share	£1.50

Conclusions:

Four different valuations have emerged ranging from £1–30 asset value on a liquidation to a £2–10 value of the assets as a going concern. Although the directors of EZ are willing sellers they can not be expected to accept themselves, nor recommend to other shareholders a price below liquidation value. This therefore sets a minimum value of £1–30 per share as this can be achieved should the company stop trading and sell its assets on a piecemeal basis.

Book value of assets is not very meaningful as it does not represent the value obtainable for the assets whether it keeps going or is wound up. The going concern value of assets would be more appropriate if the company was using these assets to full effect. A 20% pre-tax return on total assets of £1.9m suggests EZ should be earning £380,000 which is well in excess of the £275,000 actually achieved. For this reason EZ directors can not expect to receive

£2–10 per share nor would any extra payment for goodwill be justified.

Shares in similar public quoted companies can be bought on a price/earnings ratio which value EZ at £1–50 per share. Stock market prices always relate to marginal purchases and a buyer of a controlling interest would expect to pay substantially more. However, EZ directors wish to sell out and with the 6% debentures repayable in a year's time they are not in a strong bargaining position.

All things considered, it might seem appropriate to value the shares in EZ around £1–50, being more than break-up value but valuing the assets on the basis of the earnings they produce. The eventual agreement will depend on the willingness of the public company directors to buy, and the EZ directors to sell out.

Further reading

Business Mergers and Take-over Bids, R. W. Moon, Gee.
Management of Company Finance, J. M. Samuels and F. M. Wilkes, Van Nostrand Reinhold.
Merging For Profit, M. Andrews and A. Rook, Financial Techniques Ltd.

Self-check questions

1 What are the reasons for mergers and takeovers?
2 Whose clearance is required before large takeovers and mergers are allowed to proceed?

18 Company taxation

The existence of a central government with the power to levy taxes means that it can influence firms' investment decisions through the tax system. There are two aspects to taxation, one being negative and the other positive. The negative side is the payment of tax on profits whilst the positive side is the receipt of tax allowances which reduce the tax payments.

Corporation tax is the system of taxation which applies to profits of all limited companies and nationalized industries, as opposed to income tax which applies to profits of the self-employed and partnerships. Differences between the two systems are confined mainly to the tax rates and the timing of the tax payments. If we examine the principles of corporation tax first then the differences of the income tax system can be contrasted later.

There are two rates of corporation tax, either of which can apply, depending on the size of the taxable profit for the year. The normal rate is 35% at the time of writing but a small companies rate of 25% exists for firms whose profits are relatively low. There is a gradual increase in the rate from 25% to 35%, which applies to companies whose profits fall within the band where the 25% rate ceases to apply, but the full 35% rate is not yet applicable. Usually the Chancellor increases these limits in his spring budget but the actual rates of corporation tax are rarely altered. Even when they are altered it is normally too late for a company to take action as the rate of tax announced in the budget is retrospective for the tax year ending about the same time.

The accounting year for many companies will not cover the same twelve months as the tax year which runs from 1 April one year to the following 31 March. If the rate of tax did alter from one tax year to the next and the company accounting year straddled both tax years, then the year's profit is apportioned pro rata for the number of months which fall into each tax year. The two rates of tax can then be levied on the respective part of the profit which falls into each tax year as shown in figure 18.1.

Figure 18.1 Apportionment of year's profit over two tax years

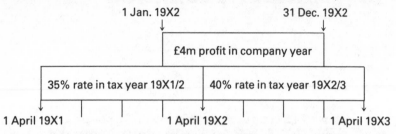

Tax payable on £4m profit $=(\frac{1}{4}\times£4m)\ 35\%+(\frac{3}{4}\times£4m)\ 40\%$

The profit on which corporation tax is levied (£4m in the example) is not identical with the profit disclosed in the firm's profit and loss account, but is an adjusted profit figure after some costs have been disallowed and some other allowances received. The statement in figure 18.2 shows the main adjustments that take place.

Figure 18.2 Corporation tax assessment

	£	£
Profit as per profit and loss account		3,940,000
add back disallowed expenses	£	
Depreciation	200,000	
Entertainment	10,000	
Political contributions	5,000	
Provision for possible bad debts	1,000	216,000
		4,156,000
Deduct		
Capital allowances		256,000
Taxable profit		£3,900,000

Corporation tax payable is £3.9m×35%=£1,365,000.

It can be seen from this statement that there are significant adjustments which affect the taxable profit. Depreciation charged by a company in its profit and loss account is added back to profit as though it had never been deducted. It is never possible, therefore, to reduce the size of the tax bill by charging extra depreciation in any one year that large profits happen to be made. Whatever figure a company charges for depreciation, the Inland Revenue will add back. The taxable profit each year comprises sales less all allowable operating costs excluding depreciation.

It would be unfair if companies were disallowed depreciation and given nothing in its place. Depreciation is the yearly charge for buildings, plant and machinery, vehicles and office equipment. The only difference between these costs, as opposed to paying for wages and materials, is the time they last. Firms could not provide goods and services to customers without investing in these physical assets, unless they chose to lease them. In this case the lease or rent payments are included as expenses in the profit and loss account and tax relief is automatically obtained.

Capital allowances

The Inland Revenue have their own system of depreciation allowances which are called capital allowances or writing-down allowances. These are available to firms which buy new physical assets of the specified categories, although some allowances are restricted to specific industries only. Figure 18.3 is a list of the rates of capital allowances at the time of writing.

Figure 18.3 Rates of capital allowances as at March 1988

Industrial buildings	4% p.a. annual allowance on a straight line basis for 25 yrs.
Plant and machinery, equipment, furniture and all vehicles	25% p.a. annual allowance on a reducing balance basis.

The capital allowances on industrial buildings are restricted to firms operating in the specified industrial classifications. The other allowances apply to all industries. From the above it can be deduced that no allowance is given for buildings used by service industries, although the equipment, furniture and vehicles they use are eligible. A deviation to this rule occurred in 1981 when new commerical buildings in 'enterprise zones' were also made eligible for capital allowances.

It may have struck you that some of these tax allowances on say plant and machinery are significantly higher than the equivalent depreciation rate used in a firm's profit and loss computations. This is because the Chancellor uses the size of tax allowances as an economic regulator and does not attempt to relate allowances to individual company needs.

Tax allowances on motor cars are most likely to coincide with the firm's practice on depreciation. Most firms use the 25% writing-down allowance on reducing capital balance when calculating their car depreciation charge to include in the profit and loss account.

Managers are no longer able to run a Rolls-Royce at the expense of other taxpayers because tax allowances are restricted to a maximum figure which effectively excludes all luxury vehicles. In the case of a car costing £8,000, the allowances shown in figure 18.4 apply.

Figure 18.4 25% capital allowances on reducing value of £8,000 car

	£
Purchase cost of car	8,000
Year 1 – capital allowance	2,000 (25% of £8,000)
Written down value – Year 1	6,000
Year 2 – capital allowance	1,500 (25% of £6,000)
Written down value – Year 2	4,500
Year 3 – capital allowance	1,125 (25% of £4,500)
Written down value – Year 3	3,375

The annual allowance falls substantially each year but the written-down value never reaches zero. Whenever the asset is sold a balancing up with the Inland Revenue takes place. If we assume the above car was sold after three years use it is unlikely it would exactly realize its book value of £3,375. If it was sold for £3,000 the Inland Revenue would give a 'balancing allowance' of the £375 difference. On the other hand if the car realized £3,800 the taxman would claim back the excess allowances of £425 previously granted. This 'balancing charge' would result in the firm paying back £425×35%=£149 tax when it settled the tax bill for the year in which the sale took place.

When appraising new investment projects the availability of these tax allowances must be incorporated in the cash flows. Tax saved by claiming these allowances will occur in the year the payment would otherwise have taken place. We must now look to see when tax is due for payment.

Tax payments

One of the good things we can say about tax on limited company profits is that it is not payable immediately, but after a time lag. The present system of corporation tax goes back to 1972 and is called an 'imputation system'. When a limited company makes a dividend payment it pays a 'net' dividend to shareholders and a tax payment to the Inland Revenue. For example, on a net dividend of £750 the tax payment is £250 being equivalent to income tax at the 25%

standard rate. Such tax is deemed to be an advance payment of the company's total corporation tax liability. The shareholder receives the net dividend of £750 together with a 'tax credit' of £250, so his total or gross dividend is £1,000. If the shareholder is not liable for tax he can claim this £250 back from the Inland Revenue. Conversely, if he is liable for higher rates of tax than the 25% already paid on his behalf, he will receive a further tax bill in due course.

Most companies make two dividend payments within any twelve months, namely the interim and final dividend relating to their accounting year. This results in two payments of 'advance corporation tax' (ACT) being made. The interim dividend payment takes place after the first half-year profits are known, which may be about nine months after the start of the accounting year. The final dividend payment normally takes place after the annual general meeting has approved the directors' recommendation, which will be at least three months after the accounting year end. At this stage the total tax liability for the accounting year is computed along the lines of figure 18.2 and agreed with the inspector of taxes. The previous payments of ACT are deducted from this total tax liability to arrive at the balance or 'mainstream' tax payable. This last payment will not be due until at least nine months after the company year end, or even longer in the case of a company incorporated before 5 April 1965 when corporation tax started. It is possible for the delay to be anything up to twenty-one months after the company year end.

The nature of the above three tax payments relating to the profits of any one year makes it very difficult to generalize about exactly when tax is paid. It depends on the proportion of profit paid out as dividends as well as when the company was formed. When appraising investments we need to incorporate tax payments in the yearly cash flows. A good rule of thumb is to assume an average delay of one year in the payment of all tax on profits.

As tax payments are made in arrears, the benefit of deducting capital allowances from profits to reduce these tax payments must also be delayed. Any capital allowances a firm can deduct from its year's profit will reduce the mainstream tax payment rather than ACT payments, which are solely dictated by the size of the dividends.

In an individual project appraisal where we need to include as a cash inflow the tax saved by claiming capital allowances, it is necessary to allow either a one- or two-year time lag. This is because the investment takes place at Year O, being the beginning of the

185

project's first year. If this happened to be near the end of the company accounting year the delay could be only nine months but could, alternatively, be up to twenty-one months for a long-established company. If the investment took place at the start of the company accounting year the tax saving could be between twenty-one and thirty-three months away. Within our own company we may be able to make a more precise estimate of these delays in tax transactions.

Public authorities

Corporation tax applies to nationalized industries and they should allow for payment of tax and the benefit of capital allowances in their project appraisals. In some cases nationalized industries have large accumulated capital allowances they have not been able to offset against profits in previous years. It would be unrealistic to allow for tax payments and allowances in the normal way. If the level of future profits and the size of unused past allowances are such that it is envisaged the nationalized industry will never be liable for tax payments, then it is advisable to exclude tax completely from the cash flows. This will also be the case with local authorities, water authorities and similar bodies which are specifically excluded from corporation tax.

Income tax

Previous discussion has centred on limited companies which come under the auspices of the corporation tax system. Some businessmen trade in their own name, or as a partnership, without ever forming a limited company. Profits of these self-employed persons come under the income tax system which also applies to employees. Unlike limited companies, the self-employed do not pay dividends and any drawings or salary they pay themselves are not allowed when computing the taxable profit.

Profits from running a business are deemed to be the income of the individual or partner. Like limited companies, the various capital allowances on new investment and the stock relief system previously mentioned all apply. The remaining profits are taxed in bands at rates presently varying from 25% to 40% after the personal allowances for the particular individual have been deducted.

186

Collection of income tax from employees takes place weekly or monthly under the PAYE system. The Inland Revenue cannot operate the same system with the self-employed because the income or profits are not known until the accounting year ends. In practice it takes a few months to prepare and audit accounts, so the delay is even longer. To overcome this problem the Inland Revenue charges income tax in the current year based on the level of profits earned in the previous tax year. More precisely the normal basis of assessment for ongoing self-employed firms is to take the profits of the accounting year ended in the previous tax year as the basis for assessing tax payable in the current tax year. This is known as the 'preceding year' basis. Because current profits can never be available, tax is based on out-of-date figures. This does not mean that there is a long delay in the payment of tax but simply that current tax is based on an outdated figure. The actual payment of tax is made 50% on 1 January in the current tax year and the remaining 50% on 1 July which actually falls in the next tax year.

Taking the example of a self-employed person whose accounting year ends 31 August, the profit for the accounting year ended 31 August 1992 falls in the tax year 1992/93. This profit will be used as the basis for assessing income tax for the tax year 1993/94 which tax will be payable equally on 1 January 1994 and 1 July 1994.

When incorporating tax payments and tax savings into investment appraisals the timing must be taken into account. In the case of self-employed persons there is no delay of one year in payment, but the size of the previous year's profits determines the size of the current year's tax payment. A time lag of one year should be assumed, however, when incorporating the benefit of capital allowances into the net cash flows.

A practical difficulty occurs here when the size of the profits is such that higher rates of tax are payable. The benefit of capital allowances shows up in reduced taxable profits, starting at the highest rate of tax which would have been payable if the investment had not taken place. If the size of the capital allowance is such that a number of bands of taxable income are eliminated then the tax saved should be calculated at the different marginal rates of tax applicable in that case.

Capital gains tax (CGT)

A capital gain takes place when a possession like a building is sold for more than the firm paid for it. Such a gain is taxable at the one rate of 30%. In the case of a limited company any CGT is included in the corporation tax assessment but a self-employed person will receive a separate CGT assessment. CGT does not apply to profits made from the firm's normal trading activity but only includes profits from the sale of fixed assets and investments.

In practice firms rarely pay this tax because of 'roll-over relief' which allows them to buy new fixed assets of any kind with the total sale proceeds of the old. This defers the tax on the original capital gain until the new acquisition is eventually disposed of in its turn. As this process can be repeated without limit, CGT is not normally a problem for companies. An exception might occur on the 'sale and leaseback' of freehold premises if the firm needs the sale proceeds to pay off debts or increase its working capital, as opposed to buying new fixed assets. In this case CGT will be payable as 'roll-over relief' does not apply.

Value added tax (VAT)

This tax has little influence on business decisions although it may affect a company's cash flow. VAT is collected by the Customs and Excise in multi-stages and not just at the time of sale to the final consumer. When a firm buys goods and services it pays input tax to the suppliers as part of the invoice settlement. When the buying firm in turn sells goods or services it charges output tax to its customers, but pays only the difference between output VAT and input VAT to the taxman. Some materials may go through a number of processing stages in different firms before eventually being bought by a final consumer, so some VAT is collected at each stage. The tax point occurs at the invoice date rather than the date cash is paid in settlement of credit transactions.

It is possible for the cash flow of a firm to be adversely affected by having to pay input tax to suppliers before tax has been received from customers. This will partly depend on the credit periods for purchases and sales. Where a much longer credit period is granted to customers than is received from suppliers, the balance of tax due to the taxman may have to be paid before it is actually received.

Sales of some goods and services are zero rated, which means no

VAT is levied on the final consumer. New buildings are a case in point. Building firms will pay input tax on all building materials and services they buy in from other firms, which they then claim back from the taxman. If they pay suppliers' invoices which include VAT before they get the refund from the taxman, then their cash flow is adversely affected. It may be possible to arrange a monthly settlement in these cases in place of the more normal quarterly one.

The greatest criticism of VAT by businessmen is probably on the grounds of the extra administration required, particularly in very small businesses where office staff are minimal.

Further reading

Taxation, W. E. Pritchard, Polytech Publishers Ltd.

Self-check questions

1 Do all companies pay the same rate of corporation tax irrespective of the size of profit made?
2 Does the capital allowance on an asset in any one year always have the same value as the company's own depreciation charge?
3 If a company pays corporation tax at 35%, will the tax charge for the year exactly equal 35% of the net profit?
4 When is corporation tax paid to the Inland Revenue?
5 How is depreciation calculated on the reducing balance method?
6 How does the Inland Revenue collect income tax from self-employed persons when it does not know how much profit they made in the same tax year?
7 Do firms actually bear the cost of the VAT they have to pay on the goods and services they buy in from other firms?

19 Overseas transactions

The UK is a prominent country in international trade, exporting approximately one fifth of its total output of goods and services and importing roughly the same amount in exchange. This means that many firms are directly involved with imports and exports or own subsidiary companies which operate in foreign countries. Knowledge of exchange rates, the financing of foreign trade, the minimizing of risk and the accounting treatment of profits arising abroad is essential.

Exchange rates

When a UK exporter quotes a price to a foreign customer he has to decide whether to quote in £ sterling, in the importer's currency, or in some other recognized currency like the dollar. When quoting in sterling the exporter will know with certainty the value he will receive and be able to estimate the profit on the deal. If the exporter quotes a price in a foreign currency then his profit is subject to the uncertainty of fluctuations in the rate of exchange between sterling and that currency until the time payment is made.

Take for example a UK shoe manufacturer agreeing to sell a consignment of shoes to a French importer for 100,000 francs. At the time the contract was signed the rate of exchange between the two currencies was £1=10 francs. The importer suffers no exchange rate risk as he is paying in his own currency of francs. The exporter, however, could make a larger or smaller profit on the contract depending on what happens to the exchange rate up to the time payment takes place. Initially he expects to be able to convert the 100,000 francs into £10,000. If the rate of exchange for the £ went down to £1=9 francs the exporter would receive £11,111 on conversion of the francs. Conversely, if the £ had gone up to £1=11 francs he would receive only £9,091.

The UK abandoned the system of fixed exchange rates in favour of a floating rate in the early 1970s. Protection for importers and exporters is now more important than ever when exchange rates can fluctuate without end stops. In a recent period of four years the £ has come down from £1=$2.40 to £1=$1.46, representing a fall of 39%. This fall has not been uniform, but composed of a series of sharp movements in small periods of time. Any contract that was settled during one of these periods of violent change could have resulted in a substantially altered profit to that originally envisaged.

Minimizing risk

It appears that in foreign trade either the importer or the exporter is exposed to the risk of an adverse movement in the exchange rate. Which party it is depends on which currency is used to fix the contract price. Whether a UK firm is exporting or importing it will bear no exchange risk if the contract price is expressed in £ sterling. However, the firm is exposed to exchange risk if the contract is priced in any other currency.

Pricing in a foreign currency makes the deal more attractive to the foreign importer who knows his commitment exactly because it is expressed in his own currency. This does not necessarily mean the UK firm has to bear the risk of an adverse movement in the exchange rate until payment is received. One of the simplest and most effective ways of eliminating this risk is to deal forward.

A forward exchange contract fixes the rate of exchange now between sterling and a foreign currency, for conversion of that currency into £ at a later date, say three months or even a year hence. Depending on the time interval and which way the currencies involved are expected to move, the forward rate can be either at a discount or a premium to the 'spot rate' of exchange obtainable now.

As an example let us suppose an exporter of goods priced in dollars can obtain a spot rate of £1=$1.600 with the three-month forward rate quoted at 0.40 cents discount. By entering into a forward exchange contract with a bank he is guaranteed to be able to exchange the dollars he receives in three months' time into sterling at a rate of £1=$1.6040. Should the £ fall in value to only $1.50 during this time he would have been better off taking the risk himself as he would have received more pounds for the dollars he was paid. On the other hand if the £ rose to £1=$1.70 he would have received less pounds for his dollars. The forward exchange contract guarantees him receipt of a fixed value in pounds at very little extra cost. Such a contract cannot guarantee that the exporter would not have been better off taking the risk himself, but few would want to expose themselves to such risks in an increasingly volatile market quite outside their normal trading experience.

A variation on forward exchange contracts is possible where importers or exporters do not know the precise date of payment with certainty. They can enter into a forward exchange contract with an option to convert during part of this period. For example, a 'three months forward, option over third month' contract means that the trader can convert his foreign currency into pounds at the agreed rate at any time during the third month.

Another way to allow for exchange risk applies when an exporter expects to be paid in a foreign currency at a future date. If he borrows the same amount of foreign currency now and converts it into sterling at today's spot rate he can repay the foreign debt he incurred by the proceeds of the export contract. Provided he reinvests the loan any loss is limited to the difference between the rate of interest paid on the loan and that earned on the short-term deposit in this country. This method of exchange risk avoidance may be more appropriate to large contracts of lengthy duration.

Apart from the above risk associated with exchange rate movements, there is also the risk of non-payment for goods by a foreign buyer. The Export Credits Guarantee Department (ECGD) is a government department which acts like an insurance company and covers such risks of non-payment, thereby removing a possible disincentive to export.

Risk of non-payment may also be avoided if an exporter receives orders through a 'confirming house' which acts as an agent for overseas buyers. Such institutions may arrange for the shipment of goods to their foreign importer as well as guarantee payment to the exporter so that it is little different to a sale on the home market.

Methods of payment

For internal trade in the UK it is quite usual for credit to be granted for a period of some weeks. Normal terms in many industries are for payment to be made by the end of the month following the month of delivery, which in effect means four to eight weeks' credit.

An increasing amount of foreign trade is being conducted on this same basis being known as an 'open account'. Payment never results in the physical movement of currency but by the adjustment of bank balances in the two countries concerned. This can be effected by a Telex message or use of the slower airmail communication.

'Documentary credits' are frequently used to settle payments in international trade. Such a document is a letter from a bank to the exporter guaranteeing payment for goods on receipt of certain documents which usually include a bill of lading, invoice and insurance certificate. Payment may be immediate, or the bank may agree to 'accept' a bill of exchange, which is in effect a promise to pay at some future date, normally three months hence. The bank's acceptance of the bill guarantees its payment and it can be immediately discounted by the exporter for little more than the cost of interest for the period of waiting. In this way the exporter gets cash earlier than by waiting for the bill to mature.

When opening a credit, or accepting a bill of exchange, the bank is taking on the risk of the importer defaulting on the payment for the goods he imported. Banks will therefore approach such transactions as though they were lending money to the importer and may require guarantees or charges over company assets to secure their loan.

Financing foreign trade

In many cases exporters will view the financing of foreign trade in the same light as financing domestic trade. A mix of owners' capital and borrowed capital will provide the working capital required for both exports and domestic sales. A documentary credit or discounted bill of exchange may actually result in cash being received earlier on export trade than from sales at home.

Should further finance be required in the form of a bank loan or overdraft, the existence of ECGD insurance cover will greatly facilitate proceedings and possibly reduce the rate of interest. A variation on this theme occurs with 'buyer credit financing' where the buyer pays the exporter on delivery from a bank loan guaranteed by the ECGD. From time to time government tries to stimulate exports via special bank lending arrangements so investigation of this source is always worthwhile.

Invoice factoring is another way of financing export trade being somewhat similar to the factoring system used in the home market. Money is not advanced until the sale takes place when the factor buys the sales invoice and collects the debt from the foreign importer without recourse to the exporter. In this way working capital requirements are reduced, although not necessarily eliminated.

Exchange control

At the time of writing, exchange control no longer exists in the UK. This means that firms and individuals are free to invest abroad and firms can import goods without regard to foreign exchange availability or otherwise. This is not the case with many other countries whose balance of payments position demands that they ration out their scarce holdings of foreign currency by imposing exchange control. Such control specifies the amounts and purposes for which foreign exchange will be made available. A country may for example prohibit or impose limits on the amount of profits remittable as dividends by foreign subsidiaries to their parent company in the UK.

Separate from exchange control there may also exist a system of tariffs or quotas which prohibit or limit the importing and exporting of specified goods and services. There are international agreements specifying when, and how, such restrictions are to be used which may allow discrimination against unfair competition, the protection of developing industries or restrictions on trade for political and security reasons.

Foreign subsidiaries' accounts

Subsidiary companies operating abroad will keep their accounting records in the currency of that country. From such records the trial balance and hence the profit and loss account and balance sheet will be produced. If a foreign subsidiary's accounts are consolidated with the parent and other subsidiaries into group accounts then they must be converted from the foreign currency to £ sterling.

Assets and liabilities abroad are converted to sterling at the rate of exchange at the group year end. Due to a movement in exchange rates between the two currencies any exchange difference between yearly balance sheets is dealt with in reserves. Profits are also converted at the year end or average exchange rate, except for dividends actually remitted which should be included at the £ sterling equivalent on receipt.

The consolidation of foreign subsidiaries is something of a grey area in accounting where alternative treatment of items may be found. The precise policy adopted by a company is spelled out in the statement of accounting policies contained in its annual report.

Transfer pricing

The term 'transfer pricing' refers to the price at which goods and services are sold or transferred from one unit to another within a global undertaking. Take, for example, a holding company which owns two subsidiaries, one of which manufactures ventilation equipment whilst the other installs the same in addition to other makers' equipment. The performance of each unit, if measured in terms of return on capital, will have to take account of the transfer price of the equipment between the two units. Too low a price will result in a low return for the manufacturer and a high return for the installer, and vice versa for a price set too high. Prices should be set at normal commercial rates, that is at arm's length, but agreement on this could be a contentious point for the managers of the two units concerned.

Transfer pricing also has its relevance when holding companies trade with their foreign subsidiaries. In this case two further points will have to be considered. One relates to the level of taxation on company profits in the different countries and the tax treatment of distributed profits. It is advisable to let the bulk of the profit arise in the country where tax rates are low by transferring out at a high price or transferring in at a low price.

The other point relates to exchange control regulations. If a UK company desires overseas subsidiaries to remit dividends, but these are blocked or restricted by foreign governments' exchange control regulations, then a solution might be to transfer out at a high price. This has the effect of artificially inflating the UK parent's profits and deflating the profit of the foreign subsidiary which would not have been allowed to remit the same funds as dividends.

Obviously both UK and foreign governments are aware of these possibilities and may try to regulate such practices. Trade unions too have been known to question transfer prices from the point of view that profits are a relevant factor in pay negotiations.

Further reading

International Trade and Payments, D. P. Whiting, Macdonald & Evans.
Management of Company Finance, J. M. Samuels and F. M. Wilkes, Van Nostrand Reinhold.
The Structure of Consolidated Accounts, H. K. Jaeger, Macmillan.

Self-check questions

1 What risk does an exporter take when he prices in £ sterling?
2 What risk does the importer take on the same deal?
3 How can an exporter eliminate some of the risks involved in such trade?
4 What special sources of finance are available to exporters?
5 Why are foreign subsidiaries not always able to remit dividends back to their UK parent?
6 What does the term 'transfer pricing' mean?

Appendix 1
Manufacturing, trading and profit and loss account for the year ended 31 December 198X

	£000	£000
Sales		1,000
less Cost of sales		
Raw materials used	200	
Direct wages	400	
	600	
add Opening work-in-progress	100	
	700	
less Closing work-in-progress	200	
Prime cost	500	
add Other factory expenses	100	
Gross cost of production	600	
add Opening stock of finished goods	50	
	650	
less Closing stock of finished goods	55	595
Gross profit		405
less Administration expenses		
Salaries	30	
Printing, stationery, postages, telephone	10	
Rates, heat, light and power	10	
Bank charges and sundries	10	60
Selling and distribution expenses		
Salaries and commission	40	
Advertising	10	
Carriage and packing	20	
Motor expenses	20	90	150
Balance before charging:		255
Depreciation	20	
Auditors' remuneration	10	
Debenture interest	10	
Directors' remuneration	80	120
Net profit before tax		135
Corporation tax		60
Net profit after tax		75
Dividends		20
Retained profit		55

Appendix 2
Balance sheet as at 31 December 198X

Fixed assets	Cost £000	Depn £000	Net £000
Freehold land and buildings	40	—	40
Plant and machinery	30	20	10
Fixtures and fittings	5	3	2
Motor vehicles	10	5	5
	85	28	57
Current assets			
Stocks: Raw materials	10		
Work-in-progress	20		
Finished goods	5	35	
Debtors less provision for bad debts		30	
Cash at bank and in hand		8	
		73	
Creditors due within one year			
Finance debt	5		
Other creditors	25	30	
Net current assets (i.e. working capital)			43
Total assets less current liabilities			100
Creditors due after one year			
Finance debt (i.e. loans, debentures)		12	
Other creditors		–	
Provisions for liabilities and charges		6	18
Total net assets			82
Capital and reserves			
Called-up share capital			20
Share premium account			5
Profit and loss account			57
Shareholders' funds			82

Appendix 3
Glossary of terms

accrual Outstanding expenses for an accounting period which have not yet been paid or invoiced.

acid test ratio See liquidity ratio.

advance corporation tax A part of the total corporation tax liability which is paid to the Inland Revenue at the time a dividend is paid to shareholders.

asset Any possession or claim on others which is of value to a firm. See also *fixed assets* and *current assets*.

associated company A company in which another company owns a substantial shareholding exceeding 20% but not more than 50% of the total.

balance sheet A statement of the financial position of a firm at a point in time showing the assets owned and the sources of finance.

book value The original or historic cost of an asset less depreciation.

break-even point The level of output or sales value at which total costs equal total revenue.

budgetary control Financial plans to meet objectives in the accounting year against which actual results are compared.

capital allowance The Inland Revenue's equivalent of a company's depreciation charge. Allowances are granted on purchases of certain new assets and reduce taxable profits.

capital employed The permanent and longer-term capital used by a firm comprising share capital, reserves and loan capital in the case of a limited company. It embraces all the sources of finance excluding current liabilities.

capital gains tax The tax payable by individuals or companies on the profit made from the sale of certain assets.

capital gearing See *gearing*.

capital reserves See *reserves*.

cash flow The definition depends on the context in which the term is used but is generally regarded as the profit plus the depreciation charge for the period, on the grounds that this latter is not a cash expense.

consolidated accounts A combined profit and loss account and a combined balance sheet for a holding company and its subsidiaries.

contribution The difference between sales and the variable cost of goods sold, before charging fixed costs.

convertible loan Starts its life as a conventional loan but gives the holder the right to transfer into a specified number of ordinary shares at a later date.

corporation tax Tax levied on a limited company's profit. There is one standard rate (currently 35%) but a small companies rate applies to those companies with insufficient profit to be taxed at the higher level.

cost code A numbering system used to describe the type, source and purpose of all costs and income.

cost – direct or indirect A direct cost is one which can be specifically allocated to a product, as in the case of materials used and labour expended. An indirect cost cannot be directly related to any particular product but is more general in nature. Indirect costs are alternatively called overheads and direct costs are sometimes referred to as prime costs.

cost – variable or fixed A variable cost varies in total pro rata to the volume of production. A fixed cost stays the same total sum over a range of output levels.

creditor Anyone to whom the business owes money.

current assets Cash and other short-term assets in the process of being turned back into cash. For example, stocks and debtors.

current cost accounting A procedure for adjusting items in a company profit and loss account and balance sheet for the effects of inflation.

current liabilities Short-term sources of finance from trade creditors, bank overdraft, dividend and tax provisions awaiting payment within the next twelve months.

current ratio A measure of liquidity obtained by dividing current assets by current liabilities.

debenture A legal document acknowledging a debt by a company. It sets out details of the interest payment on the loan and the repayment of the capital. Also it will contain details of any company assets pledged as security in a fixed or floating charge.

debtor A credit customer or other party who owes money to the firm.

debt ratio The relationship of total debts to total assets.

deferred tax Tax which is not payable at one specific time but which may become payable at a future date.

depreciation A proportion of the original or current cost of a fixed asset which is charged as an expense in a company profit and loss account.

discounted cash flow yield A measure of the true rate of profitability expected on a project. It represents the maximum rate of interest which could be paid on the diminishing capital balance of an investment.

dividend A periodic profit distribution to shareholders in proportion to the amount of shares held.

dividend cover A measure of the security of the dividend payment obtained by dividing the profit after tax by the total dividend.

dividend yield The income obtained from the gross dividend as a percentage of the current market price of a share.

double entry bookkeeping The method of recording financial transactions whereby every item is entered as a debit in one account and a corresponding credit in another.

earnings yield The earnings per share expressed as a percentage of the current market price of an ordinary share.

equity See *shareholders' funds*.

factoring The acquisition of finance from a specialist company against the security of sales invoices which that company collects.

fixed assets Assets kept by the firm for the provision of goods or services to customers. They are not sold in the normal course of business and include buildings, plant and machinery, vehicles, furniture and office equipment.

flexible budget A budget which is constructed to change in accordance with the actual level of activity achieved.

gearing The relationship of prior charge capital to owners' capital.

goodwill The benefit accruing to a business due to its name and reputation. It is valued as the difference between the purchase price of a business and the value of the net assets acquired.

gross profit The difference between sales and the cost of goods sold before charging general overhead expenses.

gross profit margin Gross profit expressed as a percentage of sales.

group accounts See consolidated accounts.

historic cost accounting The recording of transactions at the actual cost incurred at the time of purchase irrespective of the item's current value.

holding company The parent company which owns a controlling interest in one or more subsidiaries.

income tax The tax levied on the income of employees and on the profits of self-employed persons.

inflation accounting See *current cost accounting*.

intangible assets Assets of a non-physical nature including goodwill, patents, trade marks and royalty agreements.

invoice discounting A form of factoring. See *factoring*.

liquidity ratio A measure of liquidity obtained by dividing debtors, cash and short-term investments by current liabilities.

mainstream corporation tax The balance of the tax liability after the advance payments have been made.

marginal costing A system of costing used for decision making which is based on the analysis of costs into fixed and variable categories.

minority interests The proportion of a subsidiary company which is owned by outside shareholders as opposed to the parent or holding company. Can not apply to wholly owned subsidiaries.

net profit The profit after all deductions except tax and dividends.

net profit margin Net profit expressed as a percentage of sales.

ordinary shares The class of capital entitling the holders to all remaining profits after interest and preference dividends have been paid. They are also entitled to all residual assets once other claimants have been repaid on liquidation.

overtrading A liquidity problem caused by insufficient working capital to support the level of sales.

payback period The number of years taken to recover the original sum invested.

preference shares The class of capital entitling the holders to a fixed rate of dividend prior to any ordinary share dividend. On liquidation they are also entitled to the repayment of their capital before ordinary shareholders are repaid.

present value The equivalent value now of a sum of money receivable in a later year. The net present value is the sum of all negative and positive present values in an investment appraisal indicating that project's viability when positive.

price/earnings ratio A ratio used for comparing market prices of different companies' ordinary shares. It is calculated by dividing the market price of the share by the earnings per share.

profit and loss account Sometimes called the income statement. It summarizes the income and expenditure of a company to arrive at the net profit or loss for the period.

ratio Two figures usually extracted from the profit and loss account and/or balance sheet and related together as a percentage, ratio or function.

realization An accounting concept which states that profit is earned when a sale takes place and not when cash from that sale is received.

related company A modern version of an associated company introduced by the 1981 Companies Act. It refers to a non-group company in which voting shares are held long-term with a view to exerting influence for the holding company's benefit. The holding can be any size up to 50% when it would assume subsidiary status.

reserves Revenue reserves are retained profits which can be distributed as dividends. Capital reserves are not available for distribution as they have not arisen from normal trading activities. They occur when fixed assets are revalued or sold at a profit and when a company sells new shares at a premium.

return on capital (ROC) Profit before tax and interest charges expressed as a percentage of capital employed.

rights issue An invitation to existing shareholders to subscribe for new shares when a company requires further capital.

scrip issue A free or bonus issue of new shares to existing shareholders in proportion to their existing holding. No new capital is received by the company which translates existing reserves into share capital.

share capital Money subscribed by shareholders in a limited company for ordinary or preference shares. Issued share capital is the amount of money actually received whilst authorized capital is the total amount the directors are empowered to issue at that time.

share premium account Is the excess money received by a company when it sells shares for more than their par value. It is a capital reserve and must be distinguished from the issued share capital in the balance sheet.

shareholders' funds The total amount of shareholders' investment in the company comprising both issued share capital, retained profits and all other reserves. It equals the value of all the company's assets after deducting all debts owing to outside parties. (Sometimes called the net worth.)

sources and applications of funds statement A financial statement showing the internal and external sources and uses of cash during the year.

standard costing A system of costing whereby predetermined product costs are compared with actual costs to highlight significant variances which are then investigated.

standard hour A measure of the volume of work achievable in one hour.

stock relief A tax allowance for the effects of inflation on the value of a company's stocks and work-in-progress during the year.

subsidiary A company which is controlled by another company which owns more than 50% of the voting shares.

transfer price The price at which one company sells to another in the same group.

trial balance The list of debit and credit balances on individual accounts from which a profit and loss account is prepared.

turnover An alternative word for sales.

turnover of capital The relationship of sales to capital employed, stating the number of times each £1 of capital has generated £1 of sales in one year.

value added statement A financial statement showing the wealth created by a company in a period of time and how it was distributed to the interested parties.

variance The difference between a budget or standard and the actual amount.

working capital That part of a firm's total capital which is tied up in stocks, work-in-progress and granting credit to customers. It is equal to current assets less current liabilities.

Appendix 4 Present value of £1

n Year	5%	6%	7%	8%	9%	10%	11%	12%	13%	14%	15%	16%	17%	18%	19%	20%	21%	22%	23%	24%	25%	26%	27%	28%	29%	30%	35%	40%
0	1.000	1.000	1.000	1.000	1.000	1.000	1.000	1.000	1.000	1.000	1.000	1.000	1.000	1.000	1.000	1.000	1.000	1.000	1.000	1.000	1.000	1.000	1.000	1.000	1.000	1.000	1.000	1.000
1	.952	.943	.935	.926	.917	.909	.901	.893	.885	.877	.870	.862	.855	.847	.840	.833	.826	.820	.813	.807	.800	.794	.787	.781	.775	.769	.741	.714
2	.907	.890	.873	.857	.842	.826	.812	.797	.783	.769	.756	.743	.731	.718	.706	.694	.683	.672	.661	.650	.640	.630	.620	.610	.601	.592	.549	.510
3	.864	.840	.816	.794	.772	.751	.731	.712	.693	.675	.658	.641	.624	.609	.593	.579	.564	.551	.537	.524	.512	.500	.488	.477	.466	.455	.406	.364
4	.823	.792	.763	.735	.708	.683	.659	.636	.613	.592	.572	.552	.534	.516	.499	.482	.467	.451	.437	.423	.410	.397	.384	.373	.361	.350	.301	.260
5	.784	.747	.713	.681	.650	.621	.593	.567	.543	.519	.497	.476	.456	.437	.419	.402	.386	.370	.355	.341	.328	.315	.303	.291	.280	.269	.223	.186
6	.746	.705	.666	.630	.596	.564	.535	.507	.480	.456	.432	.410	.390	.370	.352	.335	.319	.303	.289	.275	.262	.250	.238	.227	.217	.207	.165	.133
7	.711	.665	.623	.583	.547	.513	.482	.452	.425	.400	.376	.354	.333	.314	.296	.279	.263	.249	.235	.222	.210	.198	.188	.178	.168	.159	.122	.095
8	.677	.627	.582	.540	.502	.467	.434	.404	.376	.351	.327	.305	.285	.266	.249	.233	.218	.204	.191	.179	.168	.157	.148	.139	.130	.123	.091	.068
9	.645	.592	.544	.500	.460	.424	.391	.361	.333	.308	.284	.263	.243	.225	.209	.194	.180	.167	.155	.144	.134	.125	.116	.108	.101	.094	.067	.048
10	.614	.558	.508	.463	.422	.386	.352	.322	.295	.270	.247	.227	.208	.191	.176	.162	.149	.137	.126	.116	.107	.099	.092	.085	.078	.073	.050	.035
11	.585	.527	.475	.429	.388	.350	.317	.287	.261	.237	.215	.195	.178	.162	.148	.135	.123	.112	.103	.094	.086	.079	.072	.066	.061	.056	.037	.025
12	.557	.497	.444	.397	.356	.319	.286	.257	.231	.208	.187	.168	.152	.137	.124	.112	.102	.092	.083	.076	.069	.062	.057	.052	.047	.043	.027	.018
13	.530	.469	.415	.368	.326	.290	.258	.229	.204	.182	.163	.145	.130	.116	.104	.093	.084	.075	.068	.061	.055	.050	.045	.040	.037	.033	.020	.013
14	.505	.442	.388	.340	.299	.263	.232	.205	.181	.160	.141	.125	.111	.099	.088	.078	.069	.062	.055	.049	.044	.039	.035	.032	.028	.025	.015	.009
15	.481	.417	.362	.315	.275	.239	.209	.183	.160	.140	.123	.108	.096	.084	.074	.065	.057	.051	.045	.040	.035	.031	.028	.025	.022	.020	.011	.006
16	.458	.394	.339	.292	.252	.218	.188	.163	.141	.123	.107	.093	.081	.071	.062	.054	.047	.042	.036	.032	.028	.025	.022	.019	.017	.015	.008	.005
17	.436	.371	.317	.270	.231	.198	.170	.146	.125	.108	.093	.080	.069	.060	.052	.045	.039	.034	.030	.026	.023	.020	.017	.015	.013	.012	.006	.003
18	.416	.350	.296	.250	.212	.180	.153	.130	.111	.095	.081	.069	.059	.051	.044	.038	.032	.028	.024	.021	.018	.016	.014	.012	.010	.009	.005	.002
19	.396	.331	.277	.232	.194	.164	.138	.116	.098	.083	.070	.060	.051	.043	.037	.031	.027	.023	.020	.017	.014	.012	.011	.009	.008	.007	.003	.002
20	.377	.312	.258	.215	.178	.149	.124	.104	.087	.073	.061	.051	.043	.037	.031	.026	.022	.019	.016	.014	.012	.010	.008	.007	.006	.005	.002	.001
25	.295	.233	.184	.146	.116	.092	.074	.059	.047	.038	.030	.025	.020	.016	.013	.011	.009	.007	.006	.005	.004	.003	.003	.002	.002	.001	.001	.000
30	.231	.174	.131	.099	.075	.057	.044	.033	.026	.020	.015	.012	.009	.007	.005	.004	.003	.003	.002	.002	.001	.001	.001	.001	.000	.000	.000	.000
35	.181	.130	.094	.068	.049	.036	.026	.019	.014	.010	.008	.006	.004	.003	.002	.002	.001	.001	.001	.001	.000	.000	.000	.000	.000	.000	.000	.000
40	.142	.097	.067	.046	.032	.022	.015	.011	.008	.005	.004	.003	.002	.001	.001	.001	.001	.000	.000	.000	.000	.000	.000	.000	.000	.000	.000	.000
45	.111	.073	.048	.031	.021	.014	.009	.006	.004	.003	.002	.001	.001	.001	.000	.000	.000	.000	.000	.000	.000	.000	.000	.000	.000	.000	.000	.000
50	.087	.054	.034	.021	.013	.009	.005	.003	.002	.002	.001	.001	.001	.000	.000	.000	.000	.000	.000	.000	.000	.000	.000	.000	.000	.000	.000	.000

Note: The above present value factors are based on year-end interest calculations.

Appendix 5 Cumulative present value of £1 per annum

n Year	5%	6%	7%	8%	9%	10%	11%	12%	13%	14%	15%	16%	17%	18%	19%	20%	21%	22%	23%	24%	25%	26%	27%	28%	29%	30%	35%	40%
1	.952	.943	.935	.926	.917	.909	.901	.893	.885	.877	.870	.862	.855	.847	.840	.833	.826	.820	.813	.807	.800	.794	.787	.781	.775	.769	.741	.714
2	1.859	1.833	1.808	1.783	1.759	1.736	1.713	1.690	1.668	1.647	1.626	1.605	1.585	1.566	1.546	1.528	1.510	1.492	1.474	1.457	1.440	1.424	1.407	1.392	1.376	1.361	1.289	1.224
3	2.723	2.673	2.624	2.577	2.531	2.487	2.444	2.402	2.361	2.322	2.283	2.246	2.210	2.174	2.140	2.106	2.074	2.042	2.011	1.981	1.952	1.923	1.896	1.868	1.842	1.816	1.696	1.589
4	3.546	3.465	3.387	3.312	3.240	3.170	3.102	3.037	2.974	2.914	2.855	2.798	2.743	2.690	2.639	2.589	2.540	2.494	2.448	2.404	2.362	2.320	2.280	2.241	2.203	2.166	1.997	1.849
5	4.329	4.212	4.100	3.993	3.890	3.791	3.696	3.605	3.517	3.433	3.352	3.274	3.199	3.127	3.058	2.991	2.926	2.864	2.804	2.745	2.689	2.635	2.583	2.532	2.483	2.436	2.220	2.035
6	5.076	4.917	4.767	4.623	4.486	4.355	4.231	4.111	3.998	3.889	3.784	3.685	3.589	3.498	3.410	3.326	3.245	3.167	3.092	3.021	2.951	2.885	2.821	2.759	2.700	2.643	2.385	2.168
7	5.786	5.582	5.389	5.206	5.033	4.868	4.712	4.564	4.423	4.288	4.160	4.039	3.922	3.812	3.706	3.605	3.508	3.416	3.327	3.242	3.161	3.083	3.009	2.937	2.868	2.802	2.508	2.263
8	6.463	6.210	5.971	5.747	5.535	5.335	5.146	4.968	4.799	4.639	4.487	4.344	4.207	4.078	3.954	3.837	3.726	3.619	3.518	3.421	3.329	3.241	3.156	3.076	2.999	2.925	2.598	2.331
9	7.108	6.802	6.515	6.247	5.995	5.759	5.537	5.328	5.132	4.946	4.772	4.607	4.451	4.303	4.163	4.031	3.905	3.786	3.673	3.566	3.463	3.366	3.273	3.184	3.100	3.019	2.665	2.379
10	7.722	7.360	7.024	6.710	6.418	6.145	5.889	5.650	5.426	5.216	5.019	4.833	4.659	4.494	4.339	4.192	4.054	3.923	3.799	3.682	3.571	3.465	3.364	3.269	3.178	3.092	2.715	2.414
11	8.306	7.887	7.499	7.139	6.805	6.495	6.207	5.938	5.687	5.453	5.234	5.029	4.836	4.656	4.486	4.327	4.177	4.035	3.902	3.776	3.656	3.544	3.437	3.335	3.239	3.147	2.752	2.438
12	8.863	8.384	7.943	7.536	7.161	6.814	6.492	6.194	5.918	5.660	5.421	5.197	4.988	4.793	4.611	4.439	4.278	4.127	3.985	3.851	3.725	3.606	3.493	3.387	3.286	3.190	2.779	2.456
13	9.394	8.853	8.358	7.904	7.487	7.103	6.750	6.424	6.122	5.842	5.583	5.342	5.118	4.910	4.715	4.533	4.362	4.203	4.053	3.912	3.780	3.656	3.538	3.427	3.322	3.223	2.799	2.469
14	9.899	9.295	8.745	8.244	7.786	7.367	6.982	6.628	6.302	6.002	5.724	5.468	5.229	5.008	4.802	4.611	4.432	4.265	4.108	3.962	3.824	3.695	3.573	3.459	3.351	3.249	2.814	2.478
15	10.380	9.712	9.108	8.559	8.061	7.606	7.191	6.811	6.462	6.142	5.847	5.575	5.324	5.092	4.876	4.675	4.490	4.315	4.153	4.001	3.859	3.726	3.601	3.483	3.373	3.268	2.825	2.484
16	10.838	10.106	9.447	8.851	8.313	7.824	7.379	6.974	6.604	6.265	5.954	5.669	5.405	5.162	4.938	4.730	4.536	4.357	4.190	4.033	3.887	3.751	3.623	3.503	3.390	3.283	2.834	2.489
17	11.274	10.477	9.763	9.122	8.544	8.022	7.549	7.120	6.729	6.373	6.047	5.749	5.475	5.222	4.990	4.775	4.576	4.391	4.219	4.059	3.910	3.771	3.640	3.518	3.403	3.295	2.840	2.492
18	11.690	10.828	10.059	9.372	8.756	8.201	7.702	7.250	6.840	6.467	6.128	5.818	5.534	5.273	5.033	4.812	4.608	4.419	4.243	4.080	3.928	3.786	3.654	3.529	3.413	3.304	2.844	2.494
19	12.085	11.158	10.336	9.604	8.950	8.365	7.839	7.366	6.938	6.550	6.198	5.877	5.584	5.316	5.070	4.844	4.635	4.442	4.263	4.097	3.942	3.799	3.666	3.539	3.421	3.311	2.848	2.496
20	12.462	11.470	10.594	9.818	9.129	8.514	7.963	7.469	7.025	6.623	6.259	5.929	5.628	5.353	5.101	4.870	4.657	4.460	4.279	4.110	3.954	3.808	3.673	3.546	3.427	3.316	2.850	2.497
25	14.094	12.783	11.654	10.675	9.823	9.077	8.422	7.843	7.330	6.873	6.464	6.097	5.766	5.467	5.195	4.948	4.721	4.514	4.323	4.147	3.985	3.834	3.694	3.564	3.442	3.329	2.856	2.499
30	15.372	13.765	12.409	11.258	10.274	9.427	8.694	8.055	7.496	7.003	6.566	6.177	5.829	5.517	5.235	4.979	4.746	4.534	4.339	4.160	3.995	3.842	3.701	3.569	3.447	3.332	2.857	2.500
35	16.374	14.498	12.948	11.655	10.567	9.644	8.855	8.176	7.586	7.070	6.617	6.215	5.858	5.539	5.251	4.992	4.756	4.541	4.345	4.164	3.998	3.845	3.703	3.571	3.448	3.333	2.857	2.500
40	17.159	15.046	13.332	11.925	10.757	9.779	8.951	8.244	7.634	7.105	6.642	6.234	5.871	5.548	5.258	4.997	4.760	4.544	4.347	4.166	3.999	3.846	3.703	3.571	3.448	3.333	2.857	2.500
45	17.774	15.456	13.606	12.108	10.881	9.863	9.008	8.283	7.661	7.123	6.654	6.242	5.877	5.552	5.261	4.999	4.761	4.545	4.347	4.166	4.000	3.846	3.704	3.571	3.448	3.333	2.857	2.500
50	18.256	15.762	13.801	12.234	10.962	9.915	9.042	8.305	7.675	7.133	6.661	6.246	5.880	5.554	5.262	5.000	4.762	4.545	4.348	4.167	4.000	3.846	3.704	3.571	3.448	3.333	2.857	2.500

Note: The above present value factors are based on year-end interest calculations.

Appendix 6 Statements of standard accounting practice as at March 1987

SSAP no.	Topic	Issued
1	*Accounting for Associated Companies* – deals with the accounting treatment of substantial (20–50%) investments in other companies which are not subsidiaries.	1971 1982 (rev.)
2	*Disclosure of Accounting Policies* – details the accounting concepts, bases and policies which should be disclosed in the annual accounts.	1971 1973 (rev.)
3	*Earnings per Share* – defines the method of calculation to be used with particular reference to corporation tax and the number of shares issued.	1972 1974 (rev.)
4	*The Accounting Treatment of Government Grants* – states two methods of dealing with grants towards capital expenditure and how they are to be credited to revenue over the asset's life.	1974
5	*Accounting for Value Added Tax* – states that sales turnover shown in the profit and loss account should exclude VAT and that any fixed assets should include any related irrecoverable VAT.	1974
6	*Extraordinary Items and Prior Year Adjustments* – deals with their accounting treatment in the profit and loss account and balance sheet.	1975 1975 (rev.)
8	*The Treatment of Taxation* – under the imputation system of corporation tax – details to be shown in the profit and loss account and balance sheet.	1974 1977 (rev.)
9	*Stocks and Work-in-progress* – states the basis on which these items, including long-term contract work, are to be valued for balance sheet purposes together with disclosure of the policies followed.	1975 1980 (rev.)
10	*Statements of Sources and Applications of Funds* – lays down the format in which such statements are to be presented in published accounts.	1975
12	*Accounting for Depreciation* – details the basis on which depreciation is to be calculated and the information to be disclosed in the annual accounts.	1977 1987 (rev.)
13	*Accounting for Research and Development* – states that fixed assets used for research and development facilities	1977

are to be depreciated over their expected life but other expenditure should normally be charged to the profit and loss account when incurred.

14 *Group Accounts* – builds on the legal requirements to produce consolidated accounts. 1978

15 *Accounting for Deferred Taxation* – specifies deferred taxation should be accounted for where profit in the profit and loss account differs from profit for taxation purposes. 1978 / 1985 (rev.)

16 *Current Cost Accounting* – specifies how larger companies (as defined) should produce supplementary profit and loss account and balance sheet statements showing the effects of inflation on profit and asset values. Not mandatory after 1985. 1980 / 1985 (rev.)

17 *Accounting for Post-Balance Sheet Events* – states when subsequent events should be disclosed in prior period financial statements. 1980

18 *Accounting for Contingencies* – requires the disclosure of material contingent losses. 1980

19 *Accounting for Investment Properties* – states that such investments (excluding medium-term leaseholds) should not be depreciated but shown at open market value with changes in value incorporated in a special revaluation reserve. 1981

20 *Foreign Currency Translation* – specifies how transactions in a foreign currency are to be exchanged into £ sterling. 1983

21 *Accounting for Leases and HP Contracts* – differentiates finance leases from operating leases and states the accounting treatment of assets and liabilities in the accounts of lessors and lessees. 1984

22 *Accounting for Goodwill* – states that any purchased goodwill should be written off against reserves immediately but may alternatively be written off against ordinary profits over a number of years. 1984

23 *Accounting for Aquisitions and Mergers* – differentiates acquisition accounting from merger accounting and states the basis on which assets and liabilities are brought into group accounts. Is additional to requirements of SSAP 14. 1985

Appendix 7
Answers to self-check questions

Chapter 1

1 (a) Each business is regarded as a *separate entity*.
  (b) Only transactions which have a *money measurement* can be recorded.
  (c) Each transaction is entered twice under the system of *double entry* bookkeeping.
  (d) *Realization* means that a sale takes place on delivery not on receipt of the cash.
  (e) *Accrual* means that expenditure incurred in the period is still accounted for when the cash payment has not yet occurred.
  (f) *Continuity* means that it is assumed the business will continue as a going concern.
  (g) *Stability* of money means transactions are recorded at their original cost to the firm.

2 Check your ideas with the accountant or the cost code manual of your firm.

3

Gosforth Gardeners' Association
receipts and payments account

	£		£
Cash at start of year	1,270	Bulk purchase of seeds, etc.	2,510
Members annual subscriptions	560	Purchase of equipment	1,500
Sales of seeds, etc.	2,250	Cash at end of year	520
Hire fees received	450		
	£4,530		£4,530

4

Bank A/C

			£
Capital A/C	1,500	Equipment A/C	1,200
Sales A/C	28,000	A. Wholesaler A/C	16,000
Balance	2,700	Van hire A/C	3,600
		Drawings A/C	6,000

Capital A/C

	£
Bank A/C	1,500

Equipment A/C

Bank A/C	1,200

Purchases A/C

A. Wholesaler A/C	17,000

A. Wholesaler A/C

Bank A/C	16,000	Purchases A/C	17,000
		Balance	1,000

Sales A/C

Bank A/C	28,000

	Van hire A/C			Drawings A/C	
Bank A/C	3,600		Bank A/C	6,000	

John Deel trial balance at year end

Bank A/C	2,700	A. Wholesaler A/C	1,000
Equipment A/C	1,200	Capital A/C	1,500
Van hire A/C	3,600	Sales A/C	28,000
Purchases A/C	17,000		
Drawings A/C	6,000		
	£30,500		£30,500

Chapter 2

1

John Deel profit and loss account for year

Expenses		Income	
Purchases	17,000	Sales	28,000
Van hire	3,600		
Depreciation	400		
Profit	7,000		
	£28,000		£28,000

Balance sheet as at year end

Sources of funds		Assets			
Capital at start of year	1,500	*Fixed assets*	*Cost*	*depn*	*net*
add Profit for a year	7,000	Equipment	1,200	400	800
	8,500	*Current assets*			
less Drawings	6,000	Cash at bank			2,700
Capital at end of year	2,500				
Current liabilities					
Creditors	1,000				
	£3,500				£3,500

2 (a) A receipts and payments account does not measure the trading performance because it does not distinguish between income and capital nor between expenses and assets. It also completely ignores credit transactions outstanding and therefore income and expenditure are incomplete. A profit and loss account is needed to measure the trading performance by comparing income with expenditure used up. A balance sheet is needed to disclose the financial position regarding the assets owned and the sources from which they were financed.

2(b)   *Mr New profit and loss account for year*

Expenses			Income		
Purchases { 20,000			Sales { 40,000		
1,000		21,000	10,000		50,000
Wages, NI, etc.		10,000	Stocks and work-in-progress		6,000
Interest on loans		2,500			
Rent and rates		7,000			
Other expenses		8,500			
Depreciation		3,000			
Profit		4,000			
		£56,000			£56,000

Balance sheet as at year end

				cost	depn	net
Capital at start of year		5,000	*Fixed assets*			
add Profit for the year		4,000	Van and plant	15,000	3,000	12,000
Capital at end of year		9,000				
Loan		15,000				
Current liabilities			*Current assets*			
Bank overdraft	3,000		Stocks and WIP	6,000		
Creditors	1,000	4,000	Debtors	10,000		16,000
		£28,000				£28,000

Chapter 3

1 Because the Inland Revenue tax the whole profit (before drawings are deducted) as income.
2 They may allow interest on capital and/or pay partners' salaries before dividing the residual profit in the agreed proportions.
3 Retained profit is the profit *after* the tax and dividend provisions have been deducted or appropriated.
4 Manufacturing, trading, profit and loss, appropriation.
5 Capital employed is the permanent and long-term capital invested in the business. In other words it is all the sources of finance excluding current liabilities.
6 Fixed assets are kept by the firm for a number of years for its own use in helping to produce goods or provide services to customers. They include buildings, machinery, vehicles and furniture. Current assets are short-term assets being cash or items in the process of being turned into cash through the trading activity. They include stocks, work-in-progress, debtors, bank balances and other short-term investments.
7 Working capital is the amount of capital employed in the current assets after deducting the short-term sources of finance, i.e. current liabilities. Therefore working capital equals current assets less current liabilities.
8 The value of shareholders' funds in subsidiary companies owned by

outside shareholders and therefore not owned by the parent or holding company.

Chapter 4

1 Preference shares are paid a fixed rate of dividend before ordinary shares and receive their capital back in full on a liquidation before ordinary shareholders are paid the balance of funds remaining.
2 Revenue reserves comprise retained profits which are distributable as dividends. Capital reserves are profits arising on the issue of new shares at a premium or the surplus on the sale or revaluation of fixed assets. Certain capital reserves are not distributable as dividends.
3 A current liability is a debt repayable within the next twelve months. Long-term liabilities are repayable more than one year hence.
4

£15,000	Cost of machine
£ 3,000	Depreciation in year one
£12,000	Written-down value after one year
£ 2,400	Depreciation in year two
£ 9,600	Written-down value after two years
£ 1,920	Depreciation in year three
£ 7,680	Written-down value after three years

5 Raw materials, work-in-progress and finished goods.
6 A provision for bad debts is the amount of debtors not expected to pay up for whatever reason. It is created by charging the estimated amount in the profit and loss account, thereby reducing the current profit figure. The provision is deducted from the value of debtors shown in the balance sheet to give a realistic assessment of the amount expected to be received in due course.
7 Goodwill is recorded only when a firm takes over another firm and pays more for the tangible assets than they are worth – the difference being a payment for goodwill. Even then firms usually write it off against profits as the value of goodwill constantly changes with the fluctuating fortunes of the company.

Chapter 5

1 A historic cost profit is calculated by deducting from income the original cost of expenses consumed in a period. A current cost profit is calculated by deducting from income the current cost of expenses consumed at the time of sale. This is usually achieved by recording all transactions at their historic cost and adjusting the resultant historic cost profit at a later stage.
2 The firm will retain insufficient cash to replenish the stocks and replace fixed assets at their inflated cost.

3 Cost of sales adjustment, depreciation adjustment, monetary working capital adjustment and the gearing adjustment.
4 Any increase or decrease in the value of an asset is matched by a corresponding change in the reserves.

Chapter 6

1 A ratio is a pair of figures extracted from the annual accounts and expressed as a ratio, a percentage or a number of times. Ratios are used to measure the profitability, performance or liquidity of a company.
2 Return on capital = profit margin × rate of capital turnover.
3 Very few ratios have an ideal value with the possible exception of the 1:1 liquidity ratio. Their use lies in comparison with previous years' ratios, with target ratios or with competitors' ratios.
4 The liquidity ratio of liquid assets/current liabilities.
5 Interest cover for Company A is 2 times and for Company B 3⅓ times. Company A is therefore more vulnerable should profits fall.

Chapter 7

1 Only a trained analyst or accountant could interpret the cash movements from a profit and loss account and balance sheet. A statement of sources and applications of funds shows the amounts of cash generated internally and raised from outside sources, leading to the disposition of that cash outside the business and into working capital.
2

Statement of sources and applications of funds – Year 2

Sources of funds		
Profit before taxation and dividend		42,000
add back Depreciation		12,000
Total generated from trading operations		54,000
Other sources		
New loans		20,000
Total sources of funds		74,000
Applications of funds		
Payment of tax	11,000	
Payment of dividend	7,500	
Purchase of fixed assets	40,000	58,500
		15,500
Increase in working capital		
Increase in stocks and work-in-progress	8,000	
Increase in debtors	12,500	
Increase in creditors	(7,000)	
Increase in liquid funds	2,000	15,500

Chapter 8

1 Value added is the wealth created by a company in a period of time. It is measured by deducting from sales the cost of all bought-in goods and services consumed.
2 A profit and loss account.
3 It could calculate ratios and compare them with previous periods, for example, added value per employee or added value/sales %.
4 The four parties to whom the value added is distributed are: employees, government, providers of capital, and the company itself.
5 Employees.

Chapter 9

1 Materials.
2 Indirect.
3 $\dfrac{£350,000}{£120,000} \times \dfrac{100}{1}\% = 292\%$ of direct labour cost.
4 (1) Floor area.
   (2) Separate meters for power. Floor area for heating, lighting, etc.
   (3) Pay roll.
5 The profit margin on sales will be 7½% which is equivalent to an 8.1% mark-up on total cost.

6

			£
Direct materials:	7.5 kg at £10.50 per kg		78.75
Direct wages:	2 hrs at £5	10.00	
	1 hr at £4	4.00	
	0.2 hrs at £3	60	14.60
Overheads	2 hrs at £50 per hr	100.00	
	1 hr at £15 per hr	15.00	
	0.2 hrs at £32.50 per hr	6.50	121.50
Total cost			214.85
25% profit			53.71
Selling price			268.56

Chapter 10

1 Firm B is cheaper for mileage under 117 per day whilst Firm A is cheaper for mileage in excess of that figure.
2 £15,000 profit.
3 Yes – the contribution of £15,000 on product C would be more than offset by the additional contribution of £24,000 on product A.
4 Yes – it is still worth tendering an even lower price which covers the direct materials cost and makes some contribution to the wages which have to be paid anyway. (Obviously firms cannot continue making such losses for long periods of time.)

5 Contribution per unit of product=£25−£14=£11.

Total contribution required=(20%×£1.5m)+£0.8m=£1.1m.

Number of sales required=$\dfrac{£1.1m}{£11}$=100,000.

Chapter 11

1 A standard hour is a measure of the amount of work which can be done in one hour under standard conditions.

2 The activity ratio relates the actual work produced to the budgeted work for that period calculated by:

$$\text{activity ratio}=\frac{\text{actual standard hours}}{\text{budgeted standard hours}}\%.$$

3 Plant layout, method study, work measurement, value engineering, value analysis, etc.

4 Adverse.

5 The labour efficiency variance compares the standard hours allowed with the actual hours taken for the work done evaluated at the standard rate per hour.

Formula: (actual hours − standard hours) standard rate.

Note: The expression within the bracket is to arrive at the difference which is then interpreted as favourable or adverse. It does not matter therefore whether standard or actual hours is placed first.

6

		(F)	(A)	
Budgeted profit for the week 1100×£6				£6,600
Variances:		(F)	(A)	
Sales price	(£32–£31) 900	900		
Sales volume	(1100–900) £6		1,200	
Material price	(50p–55p) 12,600		630	
Material usage	(12,600–10,800) 50p		900	
Labour rate	(£3–£3) 4,000	—	—	
Labour efficiency	(3,200–3,600) £3	1,200		
Variable O/H expenditure £2,100–£1,800			300	
Fixed O/H expenditure £5,700–£5,500			200	
Fixed O/H volume (1,100–900) £5			1,000	
		2,100	4,230	£2,130(A)
Actual profit for the week				£4,470

Chapter 12

1 The factor which limits or sets the level of activity for the budget period around which all budgets must be based.

2 Current level of sales; market research; sales representatives' reports; order book; seasonal trends; economic outlook.

3 A cash budget literally budgets the cash flowing into and out of a company on a monthly basis for the budget period.

4 A flexible budget calculates the costs that should have been incurred for the level of activity actually achieved and compares these costs with the actual costs to calculate variances. It therefore excludes the variances caused when actual costs are compared with fixed budgeted costs for a dissimilar level of activity.

5 Budgetary control and standard costing are both planning and control techniques setting standards of performance against which actual results are compared. This throws out variances for investigation where significant, and allows top management to practice management by exception. Their difference lies in the unit of comparison. Standard costs transcend departments and are product based. Budgets are department based and more global.

6

Closing stock	750
Production requirements	10,000
	10,750
Opening stock	350
Purchases required	10,400 kg

Chapter 13

1 High gearing is a large proportion of fixed return capital out of the total capital employed or in relation to shareholders' funds.

2 17%.

3 20% approx. (solved by calculating the DCF yield as in figure 13.3).

4 7.8%.

5
$$\text{Cost of equity capital} = \left(\frac{8p}{£1.50}\% \right) + 10\% = 15.3\%$$

6 The excess of the yield on long-dated government stocks over the average dividend yield on ordinary shares of companies.

7 14.6%.

Chapter 14

1 Expansion, new product, diversification, replacement, cost saving, alternative choice and alternative financing of investments.

2 5.6 years.

3 £2,848.

4 NPV = + £5,095.

5 21% approximately.

6 18.2%.

7 Conclusion: The investment is worthwhile as there is a surplus NPV of £299 using the cumulative PV table at 14%.

8 When an investor receives annual interest of £100 on a £1,000 investment his nominal return is 10%. If inflation exists, the real return will be less as some of the interest is needed to maintain the purchasing power of the £1,000 investment. The real return is the nominal return less the rate of inflation.

Chapter 15

1 Working capital is the amount of capital employed in the current assets after deducting the short-term sources of finance, i.e. the current liabilities. Therefore working capital is defined as current assets less current liabilities.

2 By calculating the current relationship of working capital to sales and applying that ratio to the increased sales expected.

3 N/A.

4 Bank and trade references; credit agency reports; analysis of latest annual accounts; informal grapevine through own sales representatives.

5 21% approximately.

6 83 days.

7 Raw materials, work-in-progress and finished goods.

8 Size of buffer stock; reorder level; reorder quantity.

Chapter 16

1 £1.22.

2 The advantages are that a preference dividend must be paid before any dividend is paid to other types of shareholder and in a liquidation preference shares are repaid before other shareholders. The disadvantages are that the rate of dividend does not increase if profits increase and any surplus capital remaining on a liquidation goes to the ordinary shareholders.

3 Stock market value; asset value; comparative earnings value (via p/e ratio).

4 Goodwill is the name, reputation and know-how of a firm which brings customers back and allows a firm to earn more profit than a new entrant to the industry. If one firm buys out another firm and pays more for the tangible assets than they are worth, the extra payment is for goodwill.

5 When share prices are high, price/earnings ratios will also be high. Takeovers can be financed by the issue of fewer new shares at high prices than is the case when share prices are low.

6 Market makers fix the prices at which they will buy and sell shares in a selected number of companies. Brokers act as intermediaries, or agents, between clients and the market makers, carrying out buying or selling instructions. Both market makers and brokers are members of the Stock Exchange.

7 Issue by prospectus; offer for sale at fixed price; offer by tender; introduction; placing.

8 Because the new shares are offered at a discount to the previous market price and this discount is now spread over all the old and new shares. Also because of the threat of new shares not being taken up by existing holders which will cause a temporary excess supply.

9 A scrip issue makes permanent the use of retained profits as extra share capital. It is sometimes required as a condition of a loan to safeguard the lender. Otherwise it is largely cosmetic, bringing down the market value of the shares pro rata to the size of the issue. Shareholders like more shares even though they are of the same total value. The dividend will now appear to be less per share after the issue which may help to prevent employee misunderstandings.

10 Dividend cover is the number of times the profit after tax covers the net dividend payment. The greater this figure then the more secure the dividend payment will be.

11
$$\text{Gross dividend yield} = \frac{9p \times \frac{100}{70}}{\pounds1.60} = 8\%$$

Chapter 17

1 Economies of scale through integration of the activities of the combined firms. These may be technical, marketing, managerial, financial or risk spreading.

2 Monopolies Commission.

Chapter 18

1 No – there is a small companies rate of corporation tax in addition to the standard rate.

2 No – in the case of, say, plant and machinery the capital allowance is 25% p.a. but no company will depreciate such items at that rate if they are expected to last, for example, ten years.

3 No – because of the answer in question 2, the taxable profit will only equal the company's net profit as a coincidence.

4 At the same time as dividends are paid to shareholders with the balance paid at least nine months after the accounting year end.

5 See figure 4.1 on page 52.

6 By basing the tax payment for the current tax year on the level of profit made in the accounting year ended in the previous tax year. This is known as the preceding year basis.

7 No – firms are used to collect VAT which is borne by the final consumer of the goods and services. Any VAT which one firm pays is deducted from the VAT collected from its customers and only the balance forwarded to the Customs and Excise.

Chapter 19

1 No exchange risk is involved when exporters price in their own currency.

2 The importer faces the risk that his own currency will fall in value against the £ and he will have to pay more when settlement is made.

3 If the exporter prices in a foreign currency he will be exposed to exchange risk which can be covered in the forward exchange market. The risk of nonpayment can be insured against with the ECGD.

4 Bills of exchange can be discounted immediately. Bank loans or overdrafts can be more easily obtained with ECGD cover. Buyer credit financing enables an importer to immediately pay the exporter from a loan guaranteed by the ECGD. Invoice factoring results in immediate payment.

5 Because of exchange control regulations in the foreign country or tax penalties on dividend remissions.

6 Transfer pricing means the price at which one company sells to another company within the same group. Prices can be fixed so as to reduce the overall level of taxation or help avoid foreign exchange control regulations on dividends.

Appendix 8
Further Questions

Part 1 The annual accounts

1 Claire Smith started her own business by renting a shop to hire out videos. Prepare T accounts, a trial balance, a profit and loss account and a balance sheet from the following list of her first month's transactions:

	£
Opened business bank account with	4,000
Bought shop fittings for displaying video tapes	1,000
Paid first month's rent	300
Bought stock of video tapes to hire out	2,500
Paid first week's wages	200
Banked first week's sales	300
Paid second week's wages	250
Banked second week's sales	500
Paid third week's wages	250
Bought more video tapes to hire out	600
Banked third week's sales	800
Paid fourth week's wages	250
Banked fourth week's sales	1,100
Paid electricity bill for the month	100
Paid first month's rates to local authority	150

2 Explain the precise meaning of 'profit' by reference to any relevant accounting conventions. (Essay question)

3 The following balance sheet items are in mixed-up order. Put them in groups under correct headings using the layout currently recommended.

	£
Stocks	92,825
Tangible fixed assets	116,612
Called up share capital	44,985
Cash at bank and in hand	8,632
Finance debt (due within year)	7,543
Finance debt (due after a year)	28,303
Investments (in related company)	717
Share premium account	33,891
Other creditors (due within year)	73,617
Profit and loss account	88,279
Debtors	74,402
Other creditors (due after a year)	3,525
Provisions for liabilities and charges	13,045

4 A firm buys a piece of equipment for £40,000 and expects it to last for six years after which it will be worth about £2,000. Use the reducing balance method to calculate what the balance sheet value of the equipment will be in four years' time.

5 The following annual accounts relate to an advertising agency:

Balance Sheet as at 30 April 19X7

			£000
Fixed Assets (net of depreciation)			875
Current Assets:			
Stocks and work-in-progress	310		
Debtors	770		
Bank Balance	100	1180	
Less: Creditors due within year			
Trade creditors	620		
Proposed dividend	45	665	
Net Current Assets			515
Total assets less current liabilities			1390
Creditors due after one year			
12% Debentures			700
Total Net Assets			690
Share Capital and Reserves			
Issued Share Capital			450
Profit and loss account			240
			690

Profit and Loss Account for year ended 30 April 19X7

	£000
Sales	3,100
Cost of work done	1,375
Gross profit	1,725
Overhead expenses	1,055
Debenture interest	84
Net profit	£ 586

(a) Calculate the following ratios and compare them with the trade average shown in brackets:
   (i)   Gross profit margin (50%)
   (ii) Net profit margin before interest (25%)
   (iii) Return on capital employed (35%)
   (iv) Turnover of capital (1.4 times)
   (v) Current ratio (2.2:1)
   (vi) Debtors' collection period (75 days)
(b) State whether the performance of this agency is better or worse than the trade average for each ratio and give one suggestion for improvement for each adverse ratio you find.

6 A colleague cannot understand why the firm you both work for needed a bank overdraft at the end of the year in which the firm made a record profit. You have at your disposal the following balance sheets for this year and the previous one:

	19X7	19X8
Tangible fixed assets at cost	700	868
Less: Depreciation	120	148
	580	720
Investments in new subsidiary co.	–	120
Current assets:		
Stock	160	240
Debtors	100	120
Cash	4	–
	264	360
Creditors due within a year:		
Taxation	60	40
Other Creditors	120	140
Proposed Dividend	40	20
Bank Overdraft	–	106
	220	306
Net Current Assets	44	54
Total Assets less Current Liabilities	624	894
Capital and Reserves		
Called up Share Capital	264	434
Share Premium Account	–	40
Profit and Loss Account	360	420
	624	894

Part 2 Management accounting

7 A firm plans to sell 3,000 units of its industrial suction cleaner in the coming year. Fixed overhead costs attributed to this product are budgeted to be £39,000 p.a. Direct costs per unit are:
Direct labour 3 hours at £4.20 per hour
Direct materials and components £16.26
Direct expenses £3.19
The capital employed on this production is £240,000 and the firm aims to make a 20% return on capital.
Calculate the selling price needed to achieve this objective.

8 Precision Ltd manufacture a metal fastener for the motor trade and its management want your advice. The following information is available:
(a) the product takes 12 minutes to make at £4 per hour.
(b) raw materials cost 25p per unit.

(c) Variable overheads amount to £5 per hour.
(d) Fixed overheads amount to £90,000 per annum.
(e) The proposed selling price is £2.50.
Management require you to produce the following information:
(i) A calculation of the break-even point.
(ii) A chart to illustrate the break-even point.
(iii)A calculation of the number of units needed to be sold to earn a
20% return on the £0.2m capital employed in this area.

9 Explain why absorption costing is a dangerous tool to use when
examining the effects of a change in the level of activity. (Essay
question)

10 JHL Ltd has budgeted the following figures for its three product lines
for next year:

	A £000	B £000	C £000	Total £000
Sales value	960	960	320	2,240
Variable costs	864	768	240	1,772
Fixed costs (allocated and apportioned)	48	72	100	220
Profit (loss)	48	120	(20)	148

The management of JHL Ltd are particularly concerned about Product
C and are considering various alternatives:

Alternative 1 To cut Product C's selling price by 10% which is expected
to increase demand for Product C by about 40%.

Alternative 2 To substitute a new Product D for Product C. Estimated
sales for Product D are £280,000 in the first year and variable costs are
estimated at 55% of sales value. In this case some £32,000 additional
fixed costs directly attributable to D will be incurred but £18,000 of fixed
costs directly attributable to C will be saved when it is dropped.

Alternative 3 To drop Product C completely but not introduce any new
product, nor increase sales of Product A or B. In this case the £18,000 of
fixed costs directly attributable to Product C will be saved.

Calculate the effect on the total profit of the firm of each alternative
course of action and state your preferred choice.

11 Your firm makes one-off equipment to customers' own specifications.
You have just received an order which has been costed out at £20,000
on an absorption (total) costing basis and with a 20% mark-up gives a
selling price of £24,000. The customer declines to place the order at this
price and offers to pay £19,000. Explain the circumstances that might

persuade you to accept this order at the customer's price. (Essay question)

12 The standard material cost of fabric specified for a particular garment is £4.50 comprising 3 metres at £1.50 per metre. The standard time allowed for making up the garment is 15 minutes paid at the rate of £3 per hour.

Last week 1,000 garments were made using 3,200 metres of fabric which was purchased at £1.40 per metre. The total time taken to make up these garments was 230 hours which were paid at the standard rate.

(a) Calculate the material cost variance and the material price and usage variances.

(b) Calculate the labour cost variance and the labour rate and efficiency variances.

(c) Suggest any possible reasons why these variances may have occurred.

13 The following statement shows the actual profit for one month to be less than that originally budgeted. The firm in question makes a small standardized product in large volume for use in the engineering industry.

Profit and loss account for the month

	(F)	(A)	£
Budgeted profit			10,000
Variances:	(F)	(A)	
Sales price variance	1,900		
Sales quantity variance		4,000	
Material price variance		2,000	
Material usage variance	1,500		
Labour rate variance	–	–	
Labour efficiency variance		1,600	
Variable o/h expenditure variance	200		
Fixed o/h expenditure variance	500		
Fixed o/h volume variance		2,000	
	4,100	9,600	5,500
Actual profit for the month			£4,500

You are required to give possible reasons for each of the variances disclosed in the statement and to say how they resulted in the worse-than-expected profit.

Part 3 Financial Management

14 (a) Explain the term 'Capital Gearing'.
(b) Discuss the advantages and disadvantages of a company increasing its level of capital gearing. (Essay question)

15 (a) What is the cost of equity capital that is implied in the following information?

Market price per ordinary share	£3.00
Forecast dividend per share for current year	£0.30
Recent annual growth rate of profits	15% p.a.

(b) Calculate the weighted average cost of capital using the cost of equity above and assuming a debt:equity ratio of 25:75. All the debt has a fixed rate of interest of 14% and corporation tax is currently 35%.

(c) Explain why the weighted average cost of capital is less than the cost of equity alone.

16 A firm is considering buying a machine which costs £80,000 and is expected to last five years, when its scrap value will be about £2,000 only. Taxable savings are estimated to be £40,000 each year and the rate of corporation tax is 35%. Capital allowances of 25% on the reducing balance can be claimed but no allowances are available on the £30,000 working capital required for the duration of the project. The real cost of capital is 10% and this is regarded as the minimum requirement.

(a) Set out the yearly cash flows and find their net present value using the table provided.

(b) Find the DCF yield and state your conclusions as to the worth-whileness of this project.

17 A firm is considering whether or not to replace a machine which makes metal frames for umbrellas. The remaining life of the machine is put at four years. The product sells for £2 each at a volume of about 60,000 p.a.

Three alternative courses of action have been suggested by the production engineer as follows:

A Keep the existing machine which originally cost £40,000 four years ago and is being depreciated at 12.5% p.a. on a straight line basis. The total annual cost of this method (including depreciation) amounts to £85,000 and needs the existing working capital of £25,000.

B Buy a new machine costing £250,000 less a trade-in allowance of £10,000 on the old machine. The total annual running costs would amount to £95,000 including £60,000 depreciation. Further working capital of £5,000 would be required making £30,000 working capital in total.

C Cease the manufacture of frames and sell the existing machine to another firm for £20,000 who will also pay a royalty of 20p per unit sold. Sales volume would be identical with that expected from own manufacture. The existing working capital would be recovered in full.

Calculate which is the most attractive alternative on a Net Present

Value basis if the cost of capital is 16% and state your recommended course of action.

18 New Enterprise Ltd set up in business on 1 January 1988 as a supplier of specialised chemicals to a small number of other firms. Its management have made the following plans and estimates for the year 1988:
   (a) On 1 January 1988 the company will purchase premises for £60,000 and furniture, fittings and office equipment for £16,000. The latter will be depreciated over ten years on a straight line basis but the premises will not be subject to depreciation.
   (b) Sales will be only £5,000 in January but will hold steady at £20,000 every month except in July and August when they will reach £50,000 per month.
   (c) The gross profit margin (i.e. sales less cost of sales), will be held at 40% of the selling price.
   (d) On 1 January the company will purchase £8,000 of stock and maintain this level throughout 1988.
   (e) Trade creditors demand payment on the last day of the month in which the purchase was made.
   (f) All sales are on credit and it is expected that 80% will be received by the end of the month following the month of sale, and the remaining 20% received a month later.
   (g) Overheads, wages and salaries will amount to £6,000 each month except in July when it will be double that figure. Payment of these expenses will be at the end of the same month as incurred.
   (h) There will be no tax or dividend payments during 1988.

   Prepare a monthly cash budget for the year 1988 and use it to state the amount of share capital needed to be issued on 1 January if the company is never to borrow money during 1988.

   Prepare a forecast profit and loss account for the year 1988 and a projected balance sheet as at 31 December 1988 based on the above assumptions.

   Suggest a scheme of financing (other than all equity) that may be more suitable, given the seasonal nature of the business.

19 Mr Smith is the Managing Director of Smiths Ltd, a medium-sized private company, all of whose shares are owned by himself and his wife. As he is nearing retirement age and has no family he has decided to sell out to a larger public company but is unsure of the value of his shares. The following information is available for Smiths Ltd:

Balance Sheet as at 31 December 1987

	£000		£000
Issued £1 Ordinary Shares	800	Land & Buildings	2,000
Profit and Loss Account	2,452	Plant & Equipment	1,100
	3,252	Motor Vehicles	220
10% Loan	600		3,320
Other Creditors	720	Stocks	582
		Debtors	590
		Cash	80
	4,572		4,572

The following values have been assessed by an independent valuer on a going concern basis:

	£000
Land & Buildings	2,440
Plant & Equipment	1,152
Motor Vehicles	208
Stocks	400
Debtors	480

The profit after tax and interest was £340,000 in 1987 and is expected to be about £360,000 in the current year, rising by about 5% per annum. The annual dividend for 1987 was £160,000.

The dividend yields and price earnings ratios of three companies in the same field as Smiths Ltd are as follows:

	Divd. Yield %	P/E Ratio
Company A	6.0%	8.0
B	4.8%	10.8
C	5.3%	9.7

Advise Mr Smith.

20 Explain the procedures you would adopt for credit sales in order to limit the amount of working capital tied up in debtors and to minimise bad debts. (Essay question)

Index

227

Further Reading from Kogan Page

Kogan Page publish an extensive list of books for business managers and business owners; those particularly helpful to the reader of this book are likely to be:

Be Your Own Company Secretary, A J Scrine, 1987

The Business Plan Workbook, Colin and Paul Barrow, 1988

Controlling Cash Flow, David H Bangs, 1989

Debt Collection Made Easy, Peter Buckland, 1987

Financial Management for the Small Business, Colin Barrow, 2nd edition, 1988

Funding Your Business, Kenneth Winckles, 1988

Going for Growth: A Guide to Corporate Strategy, Michael K Lawson, 1987

How to Cut Your Business Costs, Peter D Brunt, 1988

How to Deal With Your Bank Manager, Geoffrey Sales, 1988

How to Set Up and Run a Payroll System, Carol Anderson, 1990

A Practical Guide to Creative Accounting, Michael Jameson, 1987

Profits from Improved Productivity, Fiona Halse and John Humphrey, 1988

The Stoy Hayward Business Tax Guide, Mavis Seymour and Stephen Say, annual

A full list is available from Kogan Page Limited, 120 Pentonville Road, London N1 9JN.